ASPEN PUBLISHER

Friedman's
Practice Series

Property

Second Edition

Edited by

Professor Joel Wm. Friedman

Tulane University Law School
Jack M. Gordon Professor of Procedural Law & Jurisdiction

Wolters Kluwer

Law & Business

AUSTIN   BOSTON   CHICAGO   NEW YORK   THE NETHERLANDS

To contact Customer Care, e-mail customer.care@aspenpublishers.com, call 1-800-234-1660, fax 1-800-901-9075, or mail correspondence to:

Aspen Publishers
Attn: Order Department
PO Box 990
Frederick, MD 21705

Printed in the United States of America.

1 2 3 4 5 6 7 8 9 0

ISBN 978-07355-8650-5

About Wolters Kluwer Law & Business

Wolters Kluwer Law & Business is a leading provider of research information and workflow solutions in key specialty areas. The strengths of the individual brands of Aspen Publishers, CCH, Kluwer Law International and Loislaw are aligned within Wolters Kluwer Law & Business to provide comprehensive, in-depth solutions and expert-authored content for the legal, professional and education markets.

CCH was founded in 1913 and has served more than four generations of business professionals and their clients. The CCH products in the Wolters Kluwer Law & Business group are highly regarded electronic and print resources for legal, securities, antitrust and trade regulation, government contracting, banking, pension, payroll, employment and labor, and healthcare reimbursement and compliance professionals.

Aspen Publishers is a leading information provider for attorneys, business professionals and law students. Written by preeminent authorities, Aspen products offer analytical and practical information in a range of specialty practice areas from securities law and intellectual property to mergers and acquisitions and pension/benefits. Aspen's trusted legal education resources provide professors and students with high-quality, up-to-date and effective resources for successful instruction and study in all areas of the law.

Kluwer Law International supplies the global business community with comprehensive English-language international legal information. Legal practitioners, corporate counsel and business executives around the world rely on the Kluwer Law International journals, loose-leafs, books and electronic products for authoritative information in many areas of international legal practice.

Loislaw is a premier provider of digitized legal content to small law firm practitioners of various specializations. Loislaw provides attorneys with the ability to quickly and efficiently find the necessary legal information they need, when and where they need it, by facilitating access to primary law as well as state-specific law, records, forms and treatises.

Wolters Kluwer Law & Business, a unit of Wolters Kluwer, is headquartered in New York and Riverwoods, Illinois. Wolters Kluwer is a leading multinational publisher and information services company.

CHECK OUT THESE OTHER GREAT TITLES

Friedman's Practice Series

Outlining Is Important But PRACTICE MAKES PERFECT!

All Content Written By *Top Professors* • 115 Multiple Choice Questions • Comprehensive *Professor* Answers and Analysis for Multiple Choice Questions • *Real Law School* Essay Exams • Comprehensive *Professor* Answers for Essay Exams

Available titles in this series include:

Friedman's Civil Procedure

Friedman's Constitutional Law

Friedman's Contracts

Friedman's Criminal Law

Friedman's Criminal Procedure

Friedman's Evidence

Friedman's Property

Friedman's Torts

ASK FOR THEM AT YOUR LOCAL BOOKSTORE
IF UNAVAILABLE, PURCHASE ONLINE AT *http://lawschool.aspenpublishers.com*

About the Editor

Joel Wm. Friedman
Tulane Law School
Jack M. Gordon Professor of Procedural Law & Jurisdiction,
  Director of Technology
BS, 1972, Cornell University; JD, 1975, Yale University

Professor Joel Wm. Friedman, the Jack M. Gordon Professor of Procedural Law & Jurisdiction at Tulane Law School, is the lead author of two highly regarded casebooks — "The Law of Civil Procedure: Cases and Materials" (published by Thomson/West) and "The Law of Employment Discrimination" (published by Foundation Press). His many law review articles have been published in, among others, the Cornell, Texas, Iowa, Tulane, Vanderbilt, and Washington & Lee Law Reviews.

Professor Friedman is an expert in computer assisted legal instruction who has lectured throughout the country on how law schools can integrate developing technologies into legal education. He is a past recipient of the Felix Frankfurter Teaching Award and the Sumpter Marks Award for Scholarly Achievement.

CONTENTS

Essay Examination Questions

Property Essay Exam #1 2

Property Essay Exam #2 5

Property Essay Exam #3 9

Property Essay Exam #4 12

Property Essay Exam #5 15

Property Essay Exam #6 19

Essay Examination Answers

Property Essay Exam #1 24

Property Essay Exam #2 30

Property Essay Exam #3 34

Property Essay Exam #4 38

Property Essay Exam #5 43

Property Essay Exam #6 48

Multiple Choice

Answer Sheet 56

115 Property Questions 57

115 Property Answers and Analysis 88

Property
Essay Examination
QUESTIONS

PROPERTY ESSAY EXAM #1

QUESTION #1

The Federal Highway Beautification Act reads as follows:

No billboard can be placed within 660 feet of interstate highways or other highways in which the United States government pays more than 50% of the cost of building such highways, without approval of the Federal Highway Commission.

Public Interest Sign Company (hereafter PISC), a nonprofit organization, purchases land adjacent to Exit 1000 of the I-80. PISC executes leases to the following organizations permitting them to erect billboards:

I.   Borris Mart, LLC, a law firm specializing in personal injury cases. On his sign, he depicts an 18-wheeler crushing a minivan, with the words "Check with me before you take their check." His 800 number also appears.

II.   Citizens for the Fourth Amendment, a lobbying group that seeks to control police searches of cars on interstate highways. On the sign are the following words: "Just say NO to searches. Stopped by the cops? Dial 800-321-7654 before you let 'em search."

III. Swinger's Emporium, a one-stop adult book and video outlet. On the sign are the following words: "Another burger? Why not have a more satisfying break at Swinger's Emporium? Next right."

Each group applies to the Federal Highway Commission for an exemption from the Act on the grounds that the Act as applied to its organization violates constitutionally protected rights. You are counsel for the Highway Commission. Advise it as to whether the Act as applied violates the constitutional rights of any or all of the three sign lessees above.

QUESTION #2

Clifford Chump is a partner in the prestigious Washington, DC-based law firm, Chump and Chump. He owns a penthouse condo in the Beergate Building, a ten-story building overlooking Lafayette Park, right across from "the big white house on Pennsylvania Avenue." From his balcony, Chump has a wonderful view of the District, including the President's modest abode. Two months ago, Chump was catching some rays on his balcony when he noticed a gray-haired gentleman in a ten-gallon hat exiting a Black Lincoln Continental in front of the White House. Excited, he waved. Secret Service agents on the roof of the White House witnessed the scene and drew their Uzis. Four well-armed Secret Service agents charged into Chump's building, broke down the door, burst onto the balcony, and apprehended

Chump. The miserable old codger was, of course, weaponless; the embarrassed Secret Service agents apologized to him for the intrusion, citing the war on terror.

Last week Chump received a letter from the Director of the Secret Service. The director outlined his concern that important guests use the particular entrance in question to attend state dinners. He enclosed a schedule and demanded that no persons be present on the balcony two hours before and two hours after all listed state dinners. Moreover, he demanded the right to have two armed Secret Service personnel present on the balcony ten times during the next year when state dinners were scheduled.

Chump, grumpy old man that he is, dashed back a letter in which he refused to comply, arguing a deprivation of property without due process of law. He would have cited the particular amendment to the Constitution that he considered infringed upon had he recalled its number. Chump sent an interoffice memorandum that wound its way to the "takings" department, for which you clerk. Write a memorandum considering:

    I.   whether the Director of the Secret Service's request should be regarded as a taking, and
    II.   if so, what might be regarded as "just compensation."

QUESTION #3

Bernard Uchello owned a three-story house in San Francisco called the "Birdhouse." From his rooftop patio he could see, while looking north, the Golden Gate Bridge to his left and Coit Tower to his right. He passed many an evening sipping chardonnay and watching the fog settle in. In 2005, Bernard retired from his tenured position at the Coit Tower School of Law. He could no longer afford such lavish accommodations on his meager pension and decided to divide his house into two separate dwellings. He would live in the west half, the Golden Gate side, and he would sell the east half, the Coit Tower side, to some yuppie lawyer with money to burn. Bernard found his mark, and sold the right half, now called "East Birdhouse," to Huey Dewey, a wealthy new partner at the law firm of Dewey, Cheatem and Howe (apologies to "Car Talk" fans). In order to secure his view, he inserted the following clause:

> Clause 1.010.12. Vendee covenants for himself, his successors and assigns, not to build on the premises in any way that obstructs the view of the west half of the house once known as Birdhouse.

Bernard and Huey live happily as neighbors, even sharing the occasional bottle of cabernet. Alas, the stock market bust comes, and Huey is sent packing in 2008. His current job with the city attorney doesn't even reach six figures. In short, he needs to sell his half, the East Birdhouse. His broker finds a merchant banker, Alan Norris, who is still flush with cash, and Norris purchases East Birdhouse. The limitation above is not included in the deed from Huey to Norris. When Norris receives his 2008 bonus, he decides to put a deck on his roof. Uchello sees the design and objects, because once built it will limit his view to only the top third of Coit Tower.

Bernard brings an action to enjoin the building of the deck in civil district court and for damages.

I.   Should he prevail?
II. Suppose there was no Clause 1.010.12. Is there another cause of action that Bernard might bring? How would that cause be resolved?

QUESTION #4

Lisa Martin was a tenant in Pickup Truck Apartments in Boot Cut on a year-to-year tenancy that commenced in August 2007, and was automatically extended for a second year. The rent was $1,000 per month. On May 1, 2009, Lisa was lounging in her apartment watching her favorite video on MTV with her boyfriend Nate, when shotgun pellets came streaming through the ceiling, striking her in the leg and Nate in the arm. The blast came from above, the apartment of Harry Ponoroff. Since he moved in, in February 2009, Lisa's enjoyment of her apartment has been less than optimal. Harry threw wild parties on a regular basis, soirées that ended in the wee hours of the morning, and she could also hear violent fights below. When she informed the landlord, Richard Wall, of the problem, he told her that she ought to call the police. She did from time to time call the police, but the officers summoned told her to complain to her landlord. She did, and though Wall talked to Harry about the situation, the problem continued.

Although the paramedics patched her wound and that of her beloved Nate, ugly scars remained. Shortly thereafter, without informing Wall, Lisa decided to move out of the premises on June 1, and on June 30, both she and Nate filed individual actions in civil district court seeking damages in the amount of $500,000, consisting of medical bills, pain and suffering, and for the psychological trauma of having a scarred leg. In his answer, filed on July 31, Wall denied liability for the injuries to both, and demanded $2,000 from Lisa, the rent for June and July. Moreover, he asked for a declaratory judgment that the lease was extended for a further year to July 2010.

Consider the following questions:

I.   Is the landlord liable for damages as alleged?
II.   Is Lisa liable for the rent for June and July?
III. Was the lease extended, and if so, for how long?

PROPERTY ESSAY EXAM #2

QUESTION #1

Barry "Home Run King" Bonfield hit his 101st home run last night at Boot Cut Park in New Orleans, a major league record. The fat pitch was served up by Ralph "Number 13" Collins, star left-hander of the opposing team, the Slidell Yankees. Bonfield hit the homer into the bleachers where three Greenie Law faculty members were sitting swilling beer and hoping to catch a ball. The ball descended directly into the glove of Harry "Butterfingers" Ponoroff, but he (of course) bobbled the damn thing (caught it and then allowed it to fall out of said glove). It made its way into the lap of that eminent sports lawyer, Cary Roberts, who had just dozed off. Sitting next to him was Ari Vice Griffin who picked the ball out of Cary's lap and left the park smiling.

Bonfield brought an action against Griffin in conversion (a common law form of action demanding the return of personal property wrongfully taken) in the district court seeking the return of the ball, which, needless to say, is worth a pile. Ponoroff and Roberts intervened in the suit, each also demanding custody of the ball. And hang on, I believe I see Collins on his way to the courthouse, writ in hand. Not far behind him is Scott Coward, the owner of the Boot Cut Dwarfs, Bonfield's team, and also William Jefferson Clinton, the recently appointed Commissioner of Major League Baseball.

The case comes before Judge Wigan Gown, for whom you clerk. Baffled (as he always is), he asks you to write a memo considering the applicable legal theories "in play." Recall that recently he read the comic book version of Locke's *Two Treatises on Government*, so don't forget to consider the so-called labor theory of property in your analysis.

QUESTION #2

Ten years ago, Lox Cable Company purchased a right of way from George W. Lush, a recently retired federal employee, to run wires across his ranch in Crawford, Texas. The agreement was written as follows:

> For valuable consideration, the sum of $1,000,000, the party of the first part, George W. Lush, hereinafter referred to as W, covenants and agrees with the party of the second part, hereinafter referred to as Lox, that W shall permit the said Lox to erect pylons across the south 40 acres of the land known as the Ranch at Crawford which the said Lush covenants that he owns in fee simple. Said pylons shall be placed at a distance of no more than 20 yards from each other. W further covenants and agrees to allow Lox to mount utility wires on the said pylons for the operation of cable television, and to allow Lox to maintain the said pylons and wires. This covenant shall bind successors.

Immediately thereafter, Lox Cable installed both the pylons and the wires, but unfortunately its lead engineer, the European-trained Nigel Banks, placed the pylons 20 meters apart, not 20 yards (a meter is about 39 inches rather than 36 inches). Lox operated the cable system in Crawford for eight years. Two years ago, Bagel Internet purchased Lox. In addition to offering cable services to customers, Bagel also provides what is known in the trade as "high speed internet access" and local telephone service. In order to improve its "connectivity," Bagel secured the services of Cappuccino Enterprises, which installed a much larger fiber optic cable on the same pylons, but without removing the more modest cable installed by Lox. Bagel no longer uses the Lox installed wire. Once a month, Cappuccino sends an employee around to inspect the wires and pylons. In fact, last month a severe tornado decimated a couple of pylons, and Cappuccino entered onto the spread and replaced them.

Shortly after the installation of the fiber optic cable, W's cattle grazing in the vicinity of the pylons became ill. W also discovered that the new cable generated a loud hum that disturbed him while he was watching his favorite programs on the Cartoon Network in his house, which is about 15 yards from one of the pylons.

W brought an action in Crawford District Court seeking the following relief:

I.   That Bagel's use of their interest in his property be enjoined on the grounds that it constitutes a nuisance both at common law and under the Restatement (Second) of Torts (1977) §822. Alternatively, W seeks damages in the sum of $50,000 per year for the next 20 years for lost profits from his cattle-raising business and $25,000 for damage to his property.

II. That Bagel's use of its easement be enjoined and its use terminated on the grounds that the current use of the easement is inconsistent with the terms of the agreement. Alternatively, W seeks damages in the amounts set above in section 1.

III. That Bagel pay $30,000 for trespasses occasioned by its maintenance of the fiber optic wire and pylons.

So what do you think? Does W have a cause of action in nuisance or an action to terminate the easement? Argue both sides, offering competing considerations and arguments. Then assume that he does, and state which remedies a court would be likely to grant.

QUESTION #3

In 1952, Roundhead, the mayor and leading citizen of Boot Cut, conveyed one of her three mansions, called Roachacre, to the Cromwell Railway for $50,000. The deed contained the following limitation:

> To the Cromwell Railway and its heirs and assigns forever, but this interest shall cease if the Railway does not maintain rail passenger service to Boot Cut. At that time the land shall become a public park.

In 2000, the Railway sold Roachacre to Lisa Bologna for $500,000. Lisa renovated the mansion and transformed it into a high-end Italian restaurant, a venue sorely needed in Boot Cut, called Le Catanese. Two years later, the Cromwell Railway merged with Abrosden Railway and ceased passenger service to Boot Cut, though it hired Jazepea Bus Line to transport prospective passengers to and from their terminal in Bunkie, 40 miles away. Alas, demand was slack, and in May 2000, the service was discontinued.

It is now 2009. Le Catanese is so successful that Lisa appears regularly on the Food Channel, often as a guest of Emeril Lagasse. She decides to abjure the kitchen entirely and move to Hollywood, and wants to sell the restaurant to her friend Juanita, who is convinced that Honduran food is the next craze that will hit Boot Cut connoisseurs. When Juanita's lawyer searches the title, she informs her that it is possible that Lisa does not have good title.

Lisa brings an action to quiet title in Boot Cut District Court, Judge Wigan Gown (for whom you clerk) presiding. Write a memo advising the learned judge how he should decide the case.

QUESTION #4

In May 2005, Alan Norris purchased a building in San Francisco called Bank's Dreamhouse, a 15-story, low-budget hotel. Fancying himself as a West Coast Donald Trump, Norris's plan was to knock the dump down, and immediately construct on the lot a ten-story luxury apartment building called Buckingham Gate London Gardens. At the time of purchase there were no restrictions on building height in the area other than the following:

> San Francisco Municipal Code §19,765,789. All buildings primarily used for residential purposes in excess of ten stories constructed after 1990 must be erected according to standards published in Earthquake Regulation 16,345,675.

The following September, Norris hired Anne Bennatti, a world-renowned architect, to design Buckingham Gate London Gardens for $1 million. When he submitted her design for Buckingham Gate London Gardens, with projected building costs of $50 million, to the Building Inspector for approval on January 2, 2007, he was informed that there was a moratorium on constructing all buildings over five stories until earthquake ordinances were updated. Although he made frequent inquiries, it was not until January 2, 2009 that the city council acted, amending the above code section to include buildings over five stories in height. Bennatti's design did not conform to the revised Earthquake Regulation 16,345,675. Norris sought a variance from the ordinance, and it was denied. Undaunted, he reapplied for the permit, and again came up short. Reluctantly, he paid Bennatti an additional $1 million to redraft the design according to the revised Earthquake Regulation 16,345,675. The new cost of the building was $60 million, the additional $10 million due to inflation in the construction trade as well as the additional costs of making the building conform to the revised Earthquake Regulation 16,345,675.

Norris submitted the revised plans; they were approved and construction began, but work was recently halted due to the downturn in the economy. However,

Norris decides to bring an action in district court in San Francisco against the city alleging that the revised regulation constitutes a taking. He seeks from the city the following damages:

I.   The additional cool million forked over to Anne Bennatti for the second set of plans.

II. The additional cool ten million forked over to build a building that would comply with Earthquake Regulation 16,345,675.

III. The sum of $2,546,768, which represents rental profits forgone for two years, which he calculates is a loss attributable to the city for failure to issue a building permit on January 2, 2007.

Can he prevail on any or all of his claims?

PROPERTY ESSAY EXAM #3

QUESTION #1

In 2009, the Greenie Law School published a directory of its illustrious alumni. It was able to do so because the Assistant Vice Director of Alumni Affairs spent the entire summer scouring the law school records to ascertain the names of graduates, and then compiled an accurate list of their present whereabouts by "Googling" each name. The purpose of the exercise was to enable the Assistant Vice Director of Development to contact said alums in order to put the bite on them for a donation to the Weinmann Hall building enlargement project. In addition, the information was printed and bound in green leather, and offered for sale at $100, enabling the law school to make an immediate profit of $75 from each book. Wily old Professor Grouchfield, now retired, springs for the $100, scans it, reprints it, and offers for sale a leather-bound version on his web site *ripoffs.com* for $75, content to make a more modest profit of a Grant ($50) per book.

The board of trustees of Greenie Law School sue to enjoin the sale of Grouch-field's version of the alumni volume and for damages in the amount of $75 for each book Prof. G. has sold. The case comes before Judge Wigan Gown, for whom you clerk. Should the board prevail? In writing your answer, address the following:

I.   What principles of intellectual property law can be applied to this case?
II.   Can concepts derived from the law of finders and capture be applied to the case?

QUESTION #2

In late 1968, Zonoroff Inc., a mining company, opened its Toolane silver mine in the hills overlooking the City of Boot Cut. In order to reach most easily the new mine from the main highway into Boot Cut, the I-70118, Harry, chief engineer, cut a road through the grassland of Crawford Ranch, a spread of impressive size owned by Giuseppe Waldegrave Cespuglio (hereafter G. W.) in early spring 1985. The following year, Gary, Zonoroff's chief communications specialist, ran a telephone wire on poles erected through Crawford Ranch, slightly to the left of the newly cut road. Both activities were largely unknown to its owner, G. W., who was at Zale University, back East, studying International Relations and having "a ole good time," not necessarily in that order.

In 2005, after receiving his A.A. degree, cum laude, and making an unsuccessful run at national political office, G. W. returned to Boot Cut to take up ranching. In Aggie Management 101, G. W. learned (he took the course three times) that the first step a successful rancher must undertake is to fence in his spread. This he did. But when Barry, chief maintenance man of Zonoroff Inc., saw the fence, he objected because it blocked the road cut by Harry. G. W. removed the part of the fence that blocked the right of way cut by Harry, and installed locked gates at either end. He delivered a key to Cary, chief property manager of Zonoroff Inc., saying that the company could use the right of way "with his permission." Always the good neighbor, Zonoroff Inc. decided to use the more circuitous route to Boot Cut, but Cary kept the key.

It is now 2009. As you may know, the price of silver has recently gone sky high, and Ari, chief mining engineer at Zonoroff Inc., decides to increase operations. In order to do so, he brings in large earthmovers that fill a continuous stream of dump trucks that use the road through Crawford Ranch. Because silver mining has gone high tech, Ari also has fiber optic cables installed on the telephone poles, as well as high-tension electrical wires. The extensive use of the road makes it more difficult for G. W. to use the road for his feedlot operation, and the heavy loads carried by the dump trucks start to make potholes. G. W. decides to move the feedlot operation clear on the other side of his spread. To do so, he closes down the operation for two months, incurring lost profits in the amount of $20,000, relocation expenses amounting to $10,000, and $100,000 in damages incurred because of additional monthly costs of using the new feedlot over its useful life. G. W. changes the locks on the gate installed in 2005.

In June 2009, Zonoroff Inc. brings an action in civil district court to enjoin G. W. from blocking the road cut in 1985. In addition, Zonoroff seeks an order allowing it to maintain the right of way and charge the expense to G. W. G. W. resists both the injunction and the order for maintenance of the road. He demands in a counterclaim that Zonoroff Inc. remove all wires and poles from his spread. He seeks to enjoin the use of the road as such, and asks for damages in the amount of $130,000 for the telephone wires. Write a memo addressing the issues as follows:

I.   Was a property interest in Zonoroff created in the road cut by Harry? If so, when, and how?
II.   What was the legal effect of placing the gate and changing the locks by G. W.?
III. Should Zonoroff Inc. be ordered to remove the poles and wires?
IV.   If the court orders continued use of the road and Zonoroff repairs the road, can Zonoroff recoup those expenses from G. W.?
V.   May G. W. petition the court to terminate due to overuse or collect damages?

QUESTION #3

In order to stem the erosion of the banks of the Boot Cut River, the Army Corps of Engineers added in 2006 sheet steel piling to jetties on its own property. The pilings direct water downstream, and away from the river's critical fork with Toolane Creek. The result of the diversion, however, is to cause greater erosion to downstream owners, in particular, Alan Norris. The Army Corps over the last three years has attempted as part of its mitigation program to deposit land and rocks on the shoreline. Despite these efforts, the river has inundated over three yards of Norris's riparian land. Previously, Norris used the land now submerged by the diverted river water as a campground and tubing spot, yielding $50,000 per year in profit. The Army Corps projects that the water will recede over the next ten years, and the land in question will no longer be submerged. In fact, the land will eventually extend three feet into the river, enlarging the extent of Norris's property. According to experts consulted by Norris, however, it is not clear when, if ever, the land submerged will once again be dry land.

After exhausting all administrative remedies, Norris brings an action in federal district court in 2009 arguing a taking.

   I.   Consider whether, given current law, a taking has occurred.
   II. Assume that a taking has occurred; assess "just compensation."

PROPERTY ESSAY EXAM #4

QUESTION #1

Archangelo Duebomber (hereinafter Due), a survivalist, has camped on Boot Cut Stream in a remote section of Shermanfork Ranch in Texas since April 1999. As his first winter set in, Due decided to make his temporary accommodation weatherproof by building a cabin. As luck would have it, he spied a dozen white pine logs tied together with a rope floating down Boot Cut Stream. He hauled them out of the stream and worked them with his primitive tools into a comfortable cabin.

After spending some harsh years in isolation, Due decided to return to civilization and attend law school. In June 2008, short of cash, he approached Ned Shermanfork, the owner of Shermanfork Ranch, and asked Ned if he would like to purchase the cabin from him. Ned declined, and ordered Due "off my spread." Enraged at his ungentlemanly conduct, Due blasted Shermanfork with the survivalist weapon of choice, the AZ 47000. Fortunately, he only inflicted what is commonly called (in Texas) a "flesh wound." The story made the morning edition of the Boot Cut Times. Scott Coward, the lessee of Shermanfork's prime timberland, read the story and e-mailed Shermanfork, indicating to him that the logs must have been cut by Coward's men who were at the time (during the previous autumns) culling the forest and floating the proceeds down the Boot Cut River. According to Coward, the logs must have broken loose and floated into Boot Cut Stream. He demanded the use of the cabin, the return of the white pine logs, or their value. Shermanfork refused.

Due brings an action in Boot Cut District Court demanding the cabin or its value from Shermanfork, or alternatively, return of the dozen white pine logs or their value. Coward intervenes, demanding the cabin, the return of the white pine logs, or their value.

You clerk for Judge Wigan Gown. She asks you to write a brief memorandum assessing the basis for each of the three individual claims to the cabin and/or the white pine logs.

QUESTION #2

Since 1995, Richard Wall has operated a modest rooming house in the Bowery section of Swamp, populated by low-income individuals. The premises, fondly known as Wall's Flophouse, consist of a dozen one-room habitations. Last month the building was severely damaged by a fire. Reconstruction would cost $5 million; Wall is reluctant to make such investment, given that the Flophouse generated a profit last year of only $50,000. Wall pondered demolishing the structure, and he employed an architect to design a multiplex cinema for the lot; the price tag is $10 million, projected yield $250,000 per year. Last month, Wall applied to the city of Swamp for a permit to build a cinema.

The city of Swamp denied the permit, citing the Provision of Low-Income Housing Act of 2000, which provides as follows:

> Section 2,345,678. No owner or lessee of property that is devoted to the housing of low-income persons may demolish the property unless:
>
> (a) the property has been destroyed and it is infeasible to repair;
> (b) the owner or lessee has agreed to build and operate a similar number of units elsewhere in the city of Swamp; or
> (c) the owner or lessee establishes extreme hardship for an exemption from this section.

Wall brings an action in district court alleging that the ordinance is a "taking." He seeks either a court order directing the city to issue a permit, or alternatively, that the city pay damages of $10 million, the present value of his anticipated profits for the next 20 years.

The case comes before Judge Wigan Gown, for whom you clerk. She asks you to produce a memo considering:

I.   whether the Provision of Low-Income Housing Act as applied to Wall's property is an unconstitutional taking; and
II. if she should so rule, what measure of compensation she should order.

QUESTION #3

In July 2005, Jasepea Mazeratti signed a seven-year lease as a tenant in the Blissful Ignorance Shopping Center located in North Swamp. The form lease contained the following clause: "The demised premises shall be used for commercial purposes only."

Jasepea opened a fashionable Italian restaurant on the premises called "Il Spaghetteria." At first all went well. But in 2008, times become tough: spaghetti is now out. In order to cut expenses, Jasepea moved his personal belongings, and a fold-out sofa bed, into his small office behind the kitchen in mid-January.

This winter has been particularly severe in Swamp. Ice and snow removal at the Shopping Center has been spotty at best. Last month, Jasepea had to phone five times before the snowplows cleared parking spots in front of his door. When he asked the maintenance person to sprinkle de-icing pellets on the walkway in front of his restaurant daily, Jasepea found five bags of pellets in front of his door with the following written on the top bag: "Do it yourself. It ain't my job." Yesterday, Jasepea's lone customer, Beatrice Wall, slipped and fell at the entrance to the restaurant. Even though Jasepea ripped up the check, she has threatened to sue.

Jazepea has decided he wants out of the spaghetti business. He put on his snowshoes and walked across the car park to your office. He says to you, "I can't make a go of this business. I'm moving back to Sacramento.

I.   Can I get out of this lease? How? Do I need to pay the landlord anything?
II. And can Beatrice sue me? If she does, can I sue the [expletive deleted] landlord for reimbursement?"

In return for representation, Jasepea promises you pasta for life. Answer his questions.

QUESTION #4

In 2000, Alan Norris purchased a house (36 Ambrosden Avenue) in a subdivision called Ashley Gardens from Lloyd Bonfield. A person of modest income, Norris purchased property at the bottom of a very steep hill. Shortly after his purchase, Norris's house was overrun by a series of mudslides from the top of the hill, to the west of his property. To protect his house from what he regarded as his neighbor's mud, Norris contracted with an architect to build a stone retaining wall on his west boundary line. In order to further secure the wall from the frequent mudslides, the architect attached multicolored concrete beams that run from the side of Norris's house, which is about five feet from the property line, to the aforementioned wall. Norris also negotiated with his next-door neighbor (34 Ambrosden Avenue), Sal Benanatti, for the right to build a ditch on the other side of the wall (on Sal's land) in order to divert water away from the wall. A written agreement was entered into with the following terms:

> For value received, Sal Benanatti and his heirs and assigns, party of the first part, agree to maintain a drainage ditch on property known as 34 Ambrosden Avenue, in Ashley Gardens, which shall be constructed by Alan Norris, party of the second part. Said agreement shall be recorded in the Ashley Gardens Record Office.

The agreement was duly recorded, but shortly thereafter a drought began; Sal never maintained the ditch.

Last year, Sal retired to Florida, and sold 34 Ambrosden Avenue to Jesse Ventura. Jesse indicated to Norris that he found the concrete beams an eyesore, and asked him to dismantle them, citing the following clause (2,345,678) in all the deeds from the developers to first owners of the houses in Ashley Garden since its development in the 1950s:

> With the exception of stone walls no property owner may build within five feet of his or her property line.

Norris refuses, and Jesse brings an action in nuisance, or alternatively, to enforce clause 2,345,678 seeking the removal of the concrete beams.

In the course of the litigation, Jesse discovers that the wall built by Norris is actually two feet over the property line, and amends his complaint to seek its removal. He also refuses to maintain the ditch, and after torrential rains, water begins to run onto Norris's property. Norris amends his complaint, seeking an injunction ordering Jesse to maintain the ditch, and seeking to quiet title to the land up to the stone wall.

The case comes before Judge Wigan Gown, for whom you clerk. She asks you to consider each of Jesse's claims, and each of Norris's claims.

Assume the following statute is in force in Ashley Gardens:

> No person may bring an action for the recovery or possession of a property interest unless that person commences an action or makes an entry within five years after the right to commence an action or make an entry first accrued.

PROPERTY ESSAY EXAM #5

QUESTION #1

After working ten long years at the Greenie Law School, Professor Grouchfield finally earned a sabbatical. Never one to appreciate the southern climes, Grouchfield decided to spend the fall in the splendid isolation of southern Maine. He rented a mansion on a private island owned by his former Greenie dean, Jack Bob Remark. One day, while snooping around the attic, Grouchfield uncovered a musty old volume of Sir Henry Maine's Ancient Law. On the reverse side of the dust jacket, he discovered scattered notes entitled "Plot for a Movie." Grouchfield read the scribbles, jotted down notes, and called his old college roommate, Stephen Spielberg. Spielberg loved it — something about a cute little extraterrestrial who finds happiness in America — and a star is born. According to the Spielberg-Grouchfield agreement, the latter would receive $10 million if the film grossed $50 million. A scant few weeks after it is screened, Grouchfield collects $10 million in royalties and buys a vineyard in Tuscany.

Two years later, ex-Dean Remark discovered the Maine volume while browsing through his collection in Maine. As luck would have it, he noticed the scribbles. A movie afficionado, Remark immediately recognized the plot as that of *ET*. He confronted Spielberg, who confronted Grouchfield, who, as usual, shrugged his shoulders.

Remark brings an action in district court against Grouchfield and Spielberg for $50 million, the profits made on the movie. News of the lawsuit is plastered all over the media, and Richard Wall learns of the lawsuit. Wall intervenes in the suit, claiming that he owned the book and sold it to Remark; he seeks $50 million in damages.

The case with the full cast of characters comes before Judge Wigan Gown, for whom you clerk. He asks you to evaluate the legal basis for the claims of each party, and as always, he is relying on you to guide him as to which claim is the strongest.

QUESTION #2

Jasepea Maseratti owns a small home on a quarter-acre lot in Palookaville in a subdivision called Roundhead Estates. He purchased the house from Valerio Luciano, who bought the palatial dwelling from the developer, Lisa Martin. The subdivision was advertised as a "High Class Residential Community." In the plat filed in the county registry office no use limitations were noted. In the deed from Martin Associates to Luciano was the following clause:

Restrictions:

For use as a single-family dwelling.
Uses that diminish the residential character of the premises are prohibited.

When the property was sold to Maseratti no clause of restriction similar to the above was included.

Maseratti decided to build a replica of the Leaning Tower of Pisa in his front yard. He hired an architect to design an edifice to 1/10 scale or about 25 yards high. A permit was issued, and building commenced. The neighbors are not happy. They banded together and asked the city council to pass a zoning ordinance that prohibits the building of such a folly. An ordinance was proposed with the following provision:

> Towers, leaning or otherwise, may not be built on residential land in Round-head Estates.

By the time the ordinance was adopted, Maseratti's tower was nearly complete. The city council brought an action to enjoin further construction on the grounds that the building contemplated violates the ordinance. In addition, the city council raised the deed restriction mentioned above, and sought to enjoin further construction on the grounds that the building is large enough to accommodate another family and is an eyesore.

Maseratti counterclaims, seeking to enjoin the enforcement of the ordinance on the ground that it constitutes a "taking." Alternatively, if the court enforces the ordinance, he asks for compensation in the amount of $100,000 (the building costs thus far expended plus the cost to tear the tower down), with an additional $100,000 "loss of property value."

Because the case raises so many important issues at such a high level of abstraction, the case is referred to Judge Wigan Gown. She asks you to write a memorandum discussing:

    I.   Maseratti's zoning claim and
    II. the city council's attempt to enforce the servitude.

QUESTION #3

Alan Norris owns a modest shotgun house in the State of Swamp. Due to the high cost of draining land and building in Swamp, houses are rather close together. Security is a problem in Swamp, and the Stouts (who have lived in the adjacent house for the past 20 years) have decided to attach a floodlight to their house to illuminate the alleyway between the two houses (Norris/Stout). Unfortunately, in order for the floodlight to illuminate the alleyway, light must shine through the French doors at the rear of Norris's sun porch. The precise spot where the light shines in is an awkward one, because Norris has installed a golden aviary for his two rare species pet canaries right at the point of greatest illumination. The glare of the floodlight keeps the canaries awake at night (and their singing does the same for Norris). This year the canaries have failed to breed: each chick is worth $500. Although Norris has explained the situation to the Stouts, they refuse to redirect their floodlight.

A groggy Alan Norris comes into your office in May 2009 and asks you if there is some remedy. Don't suggest sleeping pills — it is a LAW office.

Assume the situation has been ongoing since May 1, 2001, and the following statute is in force:

> No person may bring an action for recovery or possession of real property unless the person who makes a claim of right has commenced an action for recovery of the real property no longer than seven years after the claim of right has accrued.

What would your advice be?

QUESTION #4

Ed Sherman loves coffee. It has been his dream to open a coffee shop in the vicinity of the Greenie Law School, and spend his infrequent idle moments dispensing coffee and ruminating on the latest advances in mediation procedures with inquiring young minds. Next door to the law school is a small house used by the university to accommodate the vice dean. Because the law faculty voted to terminate the office, it became available for rent. Sherman negotiated a five-year lease with the university commencing on January 1, 2005 with the following provision:

> Tenant agrees to use the premises only for the sale of coffee, tea, and bagels.

Sherman's business prospered, but in the following year, Buckstar, a national chain, opened a larger, more attractive facility around the corner, selling coffee and a variety of other drinks, as well as exotic pastries. Profits at Sherman's coffee shop plunged. To make matters worse for poor Sherman, a link has been recently discovered between eating bagels (which account for 94.5 percent of Sherman's profit) and various diseases, including cancer. Demand for bagels has plunged, and Sherman's business has fallen into the red. In order to improve his profit picture, Sherman began to sell croissants, and has proposed to tutor law students on the side.

Recently, however, the university's president decided that the altered complexion of Sherman's business is not conducive to the collegiate atmosphere on Ferret Street. University notified Sherman that campus security will begin to intercept trucks that deliver croissants, and should Sherman continue to provide nourishment other than in the round form with holes (and donuts don't count), University will seek to terminate the lease on the grounds that Sherman is in breach of a material provision thereof. Sherman refused to yield, and University commenced an action to terminate the lease, seeking damages in the amount of $5,000, the rental payments due under the remaining term. Sherman counterclaimed, seeking, in the alternative, either rescission of the lease or an order enjoining University from interfering with the delivery of croissants. In either case, Sherman also petitioned for the value of the lease and for lost profits.

The case comes before Judge Wigan Gown, for whom you clerk. Prepare a memorandum considering the following questions:

1. Should Greenie be able to terminate the lease and seek the rent for the entire term on the grounds that Sherman has violated an express term of the lease by selling croissants and offering tutoring?

2. Should Sherman be able to enjoin Greenie's croissant blockade, or alternatively, rescind the lease?

PROPERTY ESSAY EXAM #6

QUESTION #1

During the 1950s and 1960s, at the height of the Cold War, the United States Air Force used trichloroethylene to degrease airplane parts at Bonoroff Air Force Base near Boot Cut. To the west of the base is North Fork Ranch, which has been in the Uchello family for generations.

Until recently, the Uchellos did not graze cattle near the perimeter of the base. However, earlier this year, Carmellow Uchello, the current rancher, opened up the land immediately to the east of the perimeter to his herd of prize Sicilian cattle. Unhappily, a number of them died immediately thereafter. Shortly after learning of this unusual misfortune, Carmellow, a staunch environmentalist, had a study of the area undertaken by the prominent environmental engineering firm Hulk, Inc. The report concluded that the groundwater had been contaminated by none other than trichloroethylene from the base, which had flowed into underground cavities below his spread. The report indicated that it would take generations before the levels of contaminant would reach acceptable levels to resume ranching in the 100 acres adjacent to the base.

Angered, Uchello made an appointment with General Groberts, the base commander, to discuss compensation for his losses. He tells Groberts, "You might as well just have my land for its worth to me now." This was his second meeting with the esteemed officer. Last year he raised another point with Groberts that had irked him for some time. Even though the base is very large, the Air Force had once again begun to use an asphalt area near the base's eastern boundary as a staging ground for helicopters. Although the choppers rarely make overflights above Uchello's ranch, the noise was at times deafening. To add insult to injury, the Air Force installed a number of "Here's Johnny" chemical toilets on the asphalt staging ground. General Groberts, not known for his tact, declined to move the chopper staging ground. Indeed, Groberts subsequently moved chemical toilets two feet from the Uchello property line. While there is little odor emanating from them, in Carmellow's homespun vernacular, "They sure ain't purdy. They are a danged nuisance. I can see them from my porch."

Groberts, exhibiting his usual tact, refuses to pay for the cattle or the lost value of the land. And the noise and clutter, ditto.

Uchello comes into your office asking you if they can treat him like this. Assume sovereign immunity is not an issue. What potential causes of action might Carmellow have against the Air Force?

QUESTION #2

In 1968, the City of Boot Cut condemned a parking lot as part of its Urban Renewal Development Corporation. The lot's owner, Alan Norris, received "just compensation" from the city, including the fair market value of the lifts used to stack cars in the parking lot. The city removed the lifts, but the land remained unused for nearly 40 years, when the city sold it to the Boot Cut Law School, which began building its magnificent new state-of-the-art edifice on the lot.

Next door to the lot lived one Anne Benenatti. After Norris pulled out, Anne began parking her WV microbus on the lot. Indeed it has not moved since, except one day a week to go to church on Sundays. Benenatti frequently used the WV microbus for informal parties, particularly when her favorite team, the New Orleans Saints, was in town. Unfortunately, the spot chosen is precisely where the law school's architects have located the moot courtroom!

In addition to parking the VW microbus on the lot, Benenatti drove her Harley Davidson across the lot frequently to reach her small back garden where she kept the motorbike. Not much of a cold weather soul, Benenatti used the bike only in warm weather, which for her was May through September. This continued the practice long established when Norris owned the parking lot.

Assume the following statute is in force:

> Lands owned by the state and federal government cannot be adversely possessed, nor can land held for conservation, open space, parks, recreation, water protection, wildlife protection, and other public purposes.

Respond to the following questions:

I.   What interest or interests in property or property rights might have been acquired by Benenatti? Explain why and how (or why not) such rights or interests were (or were not) created.
II. Assume some interest or right has been created. How should she go about asserting it?

QUESTION #3

Desertacre, a 100-acre spread that bounded the Dry Gulch River to the west and federal lands at the foot of the Arid Gulch Mountain Range to the east, has been in the Nash family for generations. In 1990, the then-present occupant, Graham, decided to sell off part of the Nash spread. Because the farmstead was located on the western edge, Graham resolved to sell the eastern lands (about one-third of the spread) abutting the mountains to Collin Michael. The deed conveying the land to Michael contained the following limitation:

> The property herein conveyed is subject to the following condition, to wit, no trees or building structures may be planned or erected immediately to the east of the Nash farmstead if the trees or structure will unreasonably block the view of the property herein conveyed. Transferor and his heirs and assigns may seek an injunction whenever in the opinion of the transferor and his heirs and assigns the view will be blocked by trees or buildings.

In 2000, Michael decided to subdivide his 33-acre spread into one-acre lots. Over the past dozen years or so, Michael has transferred about half the lots subject to the following limitation:

> For residential use only. This covenant shall run with the land.

In 2005, another sale took place. Graham Nash sold the remaining acres of the Nash farmstead to Dark Southman. The following clause was placed in the deed from Nash to Southman:

> This property has the benefit of a negative easement over lands transferred to Michael in 1990 forever.

Prior to the sale to Southman, a number of two-story houses had been constructed on the lots Michael sold to others, obscuring the view of the mountains from the farmstead. Last year Michael sold the remaining lots to Onnig Enterprises, which began constructing a condo complex about eight stories high. The building is due east of the farmstead.

Consider the following questions:

I.   What interest in property was created in Nash upon the execution of the 1990 deed?
II. What interest in property was created when Nash sold to Southman?
III. May Nash or Southman enjoin the building of the condo by Onnig Enterprises?

QUESTION #4

Richard Small has lived in a palatial house at 10 Dodford Road in Boot Cut for 25 years. The house had been in his wife Beatrice's family for generations, and he moved in shortly after their marriage. Sadly, Beatrice died last year, but she left the property "to Richard Wall and his heirs for so long as he resides therein, but if he should marry or move elsewhere, to my beloved daughter Flora."

Last year the Boot Cut City Council passed an ordinance that barred persons convicted of certain prescribed sex offenses from living within 2,500 feet of a school or registered day care center. Unhappily, in his wayward youth, Small was convicted of statutory rape, an offense included in the ordinance, and served a brief term in the county jail. But since then he has been a model citizen.

Also unhappily, there is a school just down the street from 10 Dodford Lane. When the police began the process of enforcing the ordinance, Detective Brisco, whose niece Small had violated, brought the conviction to the attention of District Attorney Mc Coy. Mc Coy authorizes the police to serve notice to Small that he must leave 10 Dodford Lane by the end of the month. When Small seeks alternate accommodation in Boot Cut, he realizes that there is no accommodation in

Boot Cut that isn't within the 2,500 feet ban. He must either challenge the ban or move.

He comes into your office with two questions:

I.   Is the ordinance constitutional as applied to him;

II. and will he lose the interest in 10 Dodford Lane if he is required to move?

PROPERTY
ESSAY EXAMINATION
ANSWERS

PROPERTY ESSAY EXAM #1

QUESTION #1

I. Mart v. Commission

1. Exercise of Police Powers   The FHBA is a zoning law, and as such must be justified under the police power, the government's right to limit land use in order to protect the public from harm. Both state and federal courts have found that environmental regulation is within the ambit of the police power. Though dealing with amenities, rather than obvious danger, deference is usually given to legislatures when determining whether and how to address a potential harm to the citizenry. The Act is a valid exercise of the police power.

2. Fifth Amendment Taking   Though a valid exercise of the police power, a zoning law may clash with constitutional rights, and therefore be invalid as applied to individual conduct. Borris Mart will argue that the ordinance as applied to him is a taking of his property (his lease of the sign), which will require just compensation under the Fifth Amendment. Should he receive just compensation for the loss of his sign, and perhaps lost profits from accident victims, the court will deny his claim. A property owner will receive compensation only when his primary expectations are thwarted. When Bart leased the sign he should have known of the law. He assumed the risk of its enforcement.

3. First Amendment   Borris Mart will argue that enforcement of the ordinance should be enjoined as applied to him because it violates his First Amendment right to free speech. The court will find that his speech is commercial rather than political, and in such cases the legislature need only show that there is a rational basis for its exercise of the police power — that there is a connection between signs and accidents, and/or signs despoil the environment. However, courts protect commercial speech, but since he has other means of getting his message across, the court should uphold the law against his claim, and also deny compensation.

II. Citizens v. Commission

1. Exercise of Police Powers   As above, the FHBA is a zoning law, and as such must be justified under the police power, the government's right to limit land use in order to protect the public from harm. Both state and federal courts have found that environmental regulation is within the ambit of the police power. Though dealing with amenities, deference is usually given to legislatures when determining whether and how to address a potential harm to the citizenry. The Act is a valid exercise of the police power.

2. First Amendment   Though a valid exercise of the police power, a zoning law may clash with constitutional rights, and therefore be invalid as applied to individual conduct. Citizens for the Fourth Amendment have a strong claim to enjoin the enforcement of the FHBA as applied to them. They are exercising their free speech rights, and are also assisting others in protecting their Fourth Amendment rights. Moreover, their speech is directly linked to the conduct in question (don't let them violate your rights here and now), so it may be difficult to get their message across otherwise. It also smacks of political speech since liberal Democrats may be more interested in the search and seizure control than are conservative Republicans. The free speech claim triggers a much stricter scrutiny than that applied to property rights or commercial speech, and the court will have to decide whether the ban is absolutely necessary to protect the environment, and whether such environmental legislation is critical to protect the public from harm. The state may claim that there are other ways of getting the message across, such as leaflets in rest stops or radio spots. If the balance turns in favor of the law's validity, the court might deny an injunction; but the group's case is certainly stronger than is Mart's.

III. Swinger's Emporium v. Commission

1. Exercise of Police Powers   As above, the FHBA is a zoning law, and as such must be justified under the police power, the government's right to limit land use in order to protect the public from harm. Both state and federal courts have found that environmental regulation is within the ambit of the police power. Though dealing with amenities, deference is usually given to legislatures when determining when and how to address a potential harm to the citizenry. The Act is a valid exercise of the police power.

2. First Amendment   Although a valid exercise of the police power, a zoning law may clash with constitutional rights, and therefore be invalid as applied to individual conduct. However, the emporium may argue that its advertising is linked to free expression, erotic dancing, and literature. Were the court to concede the link, perhaps likely given Supreme Court jurisprudence, scrutiny would be of the intermediate variety. The court would require the state to demonstrate that it was not trying indirectly to regulate the conduct by banning the advertisement. In many of the erotic materials cases, the government argued that it was regulating the secondary effects of the conduct, and was therefore required to demonstrate a link between these outlets and, for example, crime. Likewise, if other advertising modes are available, it would be possible to inform travelers of the protected conduct. Government cannot ban erotic expression, but it can control time, place, and manner.

There is also a commercial speech argument, as with Mart. The legislature need only show that there is a rational basis for its exercise of the police power — that there is a connection between signs and accidents, and/or signs despoil the environment. If the court is unwilling to protect the erotic dancing on free expression grounds, which triggers a higher level of scrutiny, it is unlikely that they will buy the commercial speech argument, particularly since there are other means of getting the message across, that there is adult entertainment in the area. An injunction should be denied.

QUESTION #2

I. Chump v. Secret Service

1. Fifth Amendment Taking   This is a case of inverse condemnation. When government conduct requires a property owner to suffer a trespass, a fundamental stick in the bundle of property owner's rights, the right to exclude, has been abrogated. However, not all trespasses give rise to a "taking" requiring just compensation under the Fifth Amendment. This is a case for the application of *Penn Central*. Takings jurisprudence has focused upon two factors: (1) the character of the trespass; and (2) its economic impact. As to character, the court always finds a taking when the government requires permanent physical occupation. Chump will argue that although the Secret Service will not always be on his property, he cannot control the time, place, and manner of the physical occupation, rendering it tantamount to a permanent presence. That is a stretch, given the facts, and the court will probably regard the occupation as temporary. While the calendar is planned in advance, he will argue that his activities must be planned to coincide with the Secret Service's demands.

Chump will next argue that the economic impact of the trespass is great, that his privacy is invaded at various times, and that the value of the property to him is substantially diminished. He cannot always go on the balcony. Moreover, a prospective buyer who knew of the ongoing trespasses would be reluctant to pay the full market value of similar property situated elsewhere. The fact that only parts of his property are interfered with and that even during the invasion by the Secret Service, the interference with his property right is partial should not matter. But the court will reject the argument; as Holmes wrote in *Penn Coal,* government could "hardly go on" if it had to pay for all decreases in property values occasioned by its acts.

Chump will argue that modern cases dealing with the development of property are more careful in assessing impact. But cases like *Nollan* and *Dolan* are not on point here because there is no trade-off being requested for permission to develop. Likewise *Lucas* is inapposite because the intrusion has not deprived Chump's property of all economic value.

II. Just compensation

Should Chump prevail, he will demand just compensation. When property is taken, the government must pay just compensation. The measure of just compensation is what a willing buyer would pay a willing seller for the property taken. The calculation is difficult to make in this case. Chump will argue that the Secret Service is a tenant, and it should pay rent for the period of occupation. Moreover, each day it moves in, he is required in some sense to move out. He would calculate the rental value of his penthouse per day; add to it the cost of alternative accommodation and the expense of relocation; and suggest that such is the proper measure of damages. The Secret Service will argue that it has merely acquired occupation for a couple of hours, and that takings law does not require compensation for losses suffered by landowners, only value that has been acquired.

It would argue that a realtor should calculate the difference between the fair market value without the intrusion and the fair market value with it. That amount would likely be minimal, particularly since the emergency may not be ongoing. Its calculation will be accepted.

QUESTION #3

I. Bernard v. Norris

1. Real Covenant Running with the Land   For Bernard to prevail against Norris requires that the promise in Clause 1.010.12 run with the land. Norris will argue that the promise was not included in his deed, and even if it was, Bernard was not a party to the transfer, and therefore he cannot enforce it. Only Huey can enforce it. However, Bernard will claim successfully that the promise in the deed from him to Huey runs with the land. Though jurisdictions differ in specifics, property law has established four requirements to allow a promisee to enforce a promise made by another to be enforced against a subsequent owner, to run with the land: intent to bind successors; horizontal privity; vertical privity; and touch and concern. If met, real covenants can be enforced against successors to burdened land through damages; Norris might be able to build, but he should be required to reimburse Bernard for the lost value of his land. The requirements are:

a. Intent   The agreement specifies that successors should be bound, evincing intent that the promise binds subsequent owners.

b. Horizontal Privity   The promise was made between a buyer and a seller. Although some jurisdictions require the parties to have mutual interests in each other's land to create collateral promises with respect to land use, most jurisdictions find horizontal privity when an owner subdivides land. This is the case here. When the promise is created by those in horizontal privity, it is more certain that subsequent owners know of the restriction, since subdivision of a property is one of the time points in the change of title that attracts the attention of title searchers.

c. Vertical Privity   Vertical privity exists because the promisee and the party against whom the promise is to be enforced were parties to a legal transfer: Huey conveyed to Norris.

d. Touch and Concern   Touch and concern has many different meanings according to the jurisdiction, and the modern Restatement position abolishes it altogether. But the common thread in jurisdictions that retain it, is that the promise must confer some economic benefits to the promisee's land. This it does. The view adds value to a house.

2. Equitable Servitude   Regardless of whether the requirements of a real covenant were met, the agreement created an equitable servitude. To ask a court of equity to enjoin construction, Bernard need only prove intent to bind successors and notice. Both are present. The intent to bind successors is expressed in the transfer to Huey; and the subsequent vendee, Norris, had notice of all provisions in the chain of title. Because Norris has yet to build, an injunction is a proper remedy.

Bernard v. Huey

1. Breach of Contract Huey promised Bernard that neither he nor his successors would obstruct Bernard's view. While Bernard may sue Huey for monetary loss for breach of contract, Bernard would really probably prefer to enjoin Norris from constructing the offending building. Moreover, it may not be practical to sue Huey, who having moved, may be out of the jurisdiction, or may not be able to pay the requisite measure of damages.

II. Another cause of action

There is a reasonable nuisance claim here. Bernard would argue that under the Restatement he can show that an intentional and unreasonable invasion of his property would occur if the deck is built. Invasion of his property interest is a tough one, though he could argue that he has a "negative easement"—a sight vector to the tower—and the deck will disrupt it. This is a weak argument because courts do not usually find negative easements, though here Bernard could argue that the transfer to Huey created one by grant. The invasion is intentional. Intentional under the Restatement does not mean purposeful (that the result is desired by the actor); "knowingly" is sufficient—that Norris understands that the deck blocks the view. But Bernard must prove that Norris's conduct was "unreasonable." In seeking to enjoin the actor's conduct, the party claiming that the act is a nuisance must show under §826(a) that the gravity of the harm to him outweighs its overall social utility. Bernard will argue that the gravity of the harm is great, and that his use of the land interfered with has economic value and is well suited to the area. On the other hand, Norris will say that the deck has the same quantum of utility to him as the view has to Bernard.

If Bernard cannot enjoin, he could argue he should be compensated under §826(b). The harm is great, and Norris can compensate him for his loss: the reduced value of his land because the view is blocked. Norris needs to add that cost to the cost of construction.

QUESTION #4

I. Lisa and Nate v. Wall: Landlord tort liability

Landlords are generally not liable for damages arising from torts suffered by their tenants. The common law limited landlord tort liability to situations in which the landlord knew of a defect and concealed it from the tenant, the landlord fixed some defect poorly, or the tort occurred in common areas. This is not the case in this situation. Lisa knew about her neighbor's violent temperament, the landlord did not undertake steps to quell it, and the tort occurred in her apartment. However, Lisa will argue that the landlord had a duty to protect her and that that obligation has been breached. Courts have been more willing to extend landlord liability when a safety issue is in play, for example, where defective or inadequate locks have been provided. Lisa will argue that she informed the landlord, and he inadequately responded to her request, but absent an express promise to guard her safety, the claim is not actionable. Her remedy should be against the tortfeasor and not the landlord.

II. Wall v. Lisa: The rent

1. Constructive Eviction   A tenant is absolved of obligations under a lease if the landlord's conduct amounts to a constructive eviction. Lisa may argue that the dangerous situation amounted to a constructive eviction. Lisa must prove that the landlord had some obligation that he did not perform; that due to the omission the value of the premises to her was impaired; that the landlord had notice; and that after a reasonable time she vacated. While the landlord might not have been responsible to compensate under a tort theory, he has made an implied warranty of quiet enjoyment. While that warranty generally applies to only the landlord's own conduct, it may extend to an obligation that other tenants not disturb the peace. Lisa can demonstrate that the violent conduct was ongoing, and that the landlord had notice of the breach and failed to remedy it. She vacated on June 30, so she should argue that she is responsible only for June's rent. The difficult point would be to persuade the court that it should extend the warranty to the conduct of the landlord's other tenants.

2. Implied Warranty of Habitability   Lisa will argue that the landlord breached the implied warranty of habitability. Landlords through statutes or through reform of the common law are held to an obligation to provide premises that are fit to live in. Lisa can argue that the danger and the bullet holes to boot render the premises uninhabitable. The amount of rent should reflect the difference between its fair market value as warranted and the fair market value as is. Breach would also allow her to quit. Thus she could claim back some rent already paid, calculated as the fair market value of the premises before and after Ponoroff moved in, and be absolved of her obligation for July. Her argument is fairly strong, though the question of safety is a difficult one since it is questionable whether or not the premises were really uninhabitable.

III. Wall v. Lisa

1. Notice of Termination   Lisa will argue that her vacation of the premises and commencement of suit was sufficient to give notice that she wished to terminate her year-to-year lease as of July 31. Lisa had a year-to-year tenancy. The tenancy would continue for a further year unless either landlord or tenant gave notice that the tenancy should terminate. Thus such a short period of notice is insufficient under a year-to-year lease. Notice is a formal legal statement. Conduct is insufficient. However, the lawsuit with its various claims, including constructive eviction, filed on the 30th is likely sufficient notice. But by then it was too late; the lease was renewed. Lisa must somehow buy her way out of the extension obligation. Some jurisdictions require landlords to mitigate damages. The landlord ought to look for another tenant to replace Lisa, but she remains responsible for the rent until one is secured.

PROPERTY ESSAY EXAM #2

QUESTION #1

I. Various theories

1. Labor Theory of Property   Bonfield has a greater right to possession under the labor theory of property. Using Locke's theory, Bonfield will argue that a major league baseball is worth about $10; the fact that this particular ball is far more valuable is due to his skill and perseverance. Its value has been increased by his skill, which was honed through his labor. Griffin, on the other hand, is merely fortunate that the ball landed so close to him; his labor did not increase the value of the ball. Indeed none of the other claimants save Coward and Clinton have expended labor to increase the value of the ball. While they organized the sport, thousands of balls are knocked out of the park, and the custom is that the fortunate fan takes the ball home.

2. Law of Capture   Griffin will argue that he is the present possessor, and the ball once hit was tantamount to a wild animal returned to the wilds. Under the law of capture, he trapped, wounded, and ensnared it so as to deprive it of its natural liberty. Ponoroff and Roberts might make the same argument, but under the facts they really never had sufficient control to claim that they had trapped, wounded, and ensnared it.

Collin and Bonfield will argue that capture is inapplicable because the ball was not returned to the wild. Collins will deny that he abandoned the ball. Collins will argue that he was a possessor, and that by pitching the ball he never intended to abandon it. That won't do. Pitchers don't claim rights in the ball; nor do they expect to keep it when the ball they pitch is hit out of play. Either Collins never had possession, or if he did, he abandoned it when he threw the ball. Bonfield will claim that when he hit the ball, he had possession, and he never intended to abandon it. Again, the reasonable assumption is that balls out of play are the property of the fan who catches it. Either Bonfield never had possession, or he abandoned it.

3. Law of Finders   If capture is inapplicable, Griffin could say he is a finder, and that his right is superior to all save the true owner. Finders must come into possession of lost, mislaid, or abandoned property to have a right. Griffin will argue that the true owner has abandoned the ball; that the custom is fan's keep. Therefore his right is paramount. He found the ball in Roberts's lap. He was in the bleachers lawfully; it is a public place. Roberts never reduced the ball to his possession; therefore he cannot claim to have been the finder. Indeed he never knew the ball had landed on his lap. Likewise, Ponoroff never possessed the ball; he never caught it, which is presumably how baseballs are possessed.

QUESTION #2

I. W v. Bagel: Nuisance

The conduct of Bagel may be a nuisance if W can prove that there is an intentional invasion of W's property interest. Invasions may be non-trespassory like this one (where the intrusion is more a metaphysical intrusion than a traditional intrusion), and the invasion is intentional if the actor knows that it is likely that an invasion will occur. One need not act for the conscious purpose of causing an invasion. Finally, the intentional invasion must be unreasonable, which is defined as when the gravity of the harm of the actor's conduct to the affected property outweighs its social utility. Unlike the common law, which generally followed the first in time, first in right doctrine (W was there prior to Bagel, he may continue his conduct), the Restatement §826(a) uses an economic balancing test. W would argue that the harm is considerable: lost profits from ranching, an activity to which the land is well suited. He would also argue that high speed internet in rural areas, in the age of wireless, is not as useful to the economy as ranching. Bagel will argue progress; that the social utility of ranching is not low, but is not as great as bringing new technology to rural areas. W would respond that if the utility is high, the true cost ought to be paid by Bagel's customers, rather than free riding on W's lost property value. This argument is one better suited to Restatement §826(b). W may argue the second Restatement formulation: that the conduct is a nuisance if it is serious and the actor can afford to continue the operation and pay compensation. This argument plays into the same theme as above: why can't Bagel assume the costs of moving his operation, or compensate W for losses by passing the costs on to Bagel's customers? While W might pose the same question, it seems clear that the intentional invasion required by nuisance comes from Bagel's land use and not W's.

II. W v. Bagel: Easement

1. Initial Agreement The agreement created an easement in gross to erect pylons in a specified fashion. When an interest in property is created, and not appurtenant to the land of its holder, it is personal and is said to be held in gross. Here the easement is Lox's property, but not part of its ownership rights in land. Easements in gross, particularly commercial ones, rather like most property interests are transferable, absent express understanding to the contrary. Therefore when Bagel purchased Lox, it acquired the easement. That there was a technical error in installation should not be cause for termination of the easement. Unless the mistake was material, Bagel should continue to be able to use the easement. Depending on the jurisdiction's statute of limitations period (if ten years or less), the pylon easement might have been created by prescription. The pylons were open and notorious, and continuously on the property. But if they were there as a product of mistake, the requisite adversity might not be present. Bagel's use was permissive. However, Bagel will argue that there was no permission manifested to place the pylons incorrectly, and therefore its conduct was adverse. The prescription argument is likely to fail, but the first argument should prevail and support Bagel's claim for an easement.

2. Modernization The installation of the larger wires is likely not inconsistent with the terms of the easement. Bagel will argue that it ought to be able to modernize the easement by placing a thicker wire. The agreement is silent about the wire's girth and specific about the pylons, suggesting that the former was not an essential element of the bargain. The wires are high tension, and W may argue that it was implicit in the agreement that the use of the easement would not affect his own use of land. Still lack of specificity requires the court to consider what was in the parties' reasonable contemplation. Here modernization seems reasonable given the enterprise.

III. W. v. Bagel: Maintenance — Secondary easement

Whether inspections are also within the scope of the easement depends on the agreement. It is silent. Some courts hold that the obligation to maintain the easement falls on the holder of the servient interest: the party who owns the underlying interest in property. That avoids sanctioning trespasses on the servient tenement to repair. The holder of the servient land can service the easement while she is repairing other parts of her land. She may charge the holder of the dominant interest a reasonable share of the costs. Under this formulation, the holder of the dominant interest may compel the holder of the servient interest to maintain.

Other courts allow the holder of the easement to service. After all, she reaps the benefit of the easement. Courts then may permit the holder to enter onto servient land (the parcel subject to the easement) to maintain the easement. Here Bagel seeks only to exercise that right. The right to inspect and maintain (sometimes referred to as a secondary easement) is implied within the scope of the easement.

QUESTION #3

I. Lisa's action to quiet title

1. Nature of the Estate Limited by Roundhead   The conveyance of 1882 created a fee simple subject to an executory interest. The conveyance to an individual or corporate entity "and her/his/their heirs" creates a fee simple absolute. However, this fee simple absolute has a limitation annexed; generally such limitations are unenforceable, except those that restrict uses. These are called defeasable fee simples. Because the restriction is on land use, the limitation cuts off the fee simple not when it ceases to use the land for railroad purposes, but when the railroad no longer serves Boot Cut. It is a fee simple absolute followed by an executory interest in the city, which would presumably have the obligation to maintain the property as a park. Lisa bought the land from the railroad while trains were operating, and had good title probably until the bus stopped running, the effective termination of rail service. Even though the interest in the city may not vest longer than a life in being plus 21 years, the interest is not subject to the rule against perpetuities, because it is limited to a municipal entity.

2. Enforceability of City's Interest   Lisa may quiet title nevertheless if the court determines that the city's interest ought not to be enforced. Lisa will argue that she paid market value for the property, and the city paid nothing for its interest. The collateral act, one over which she had no control, creates a windfall in the city. Moreover, the dead hand of Roundhead ought not to be permitted to surface three score years after a conveyance. If Roundhead wanted to create a public park he could have done so during his life or at his death by will. The city will argue that the law favors charitable gifts. Moreover, Lisa could only purchase, and therefore probably paid for, only what the railroad held, a limited interest. She likely paid a discounted price. Not to enforce the limitation now creates a windfall in her.

QUESTION #4

I. and II. Norris v. City: Damages for architectural plans

In order to recover any of the three elements of damages Norris seeks, he must prove that the ordinance is a taking requiring just compensation. He must either prove that the ordinance is not a valid exercise of the police power or, if it is, that its economic impact on his property interest is greater than a private individual should bear without compensation. Both ordinances are valid exercises of the police power, because earthquakes create an even greater danger to the public when buildings are not constructed according to best practices. Norris will argue that the city ought not to be able to review its decision not to place restrictions on buildings of less than ten stories. That decision was made in 1990, and nothing has changed since then to warrant application of the standards to buildings of less than five stories. The city will argue that protection of the public from the harm occasioned by earthquakes is a valid exercise of the police power, and it ought to be free to make and revise judgments. In short, the city ought to be able to rethink its public safety policy.

The revised ordinance may nevertheless be a taking requiring the city to pay Norris just compensation. Ordinarily, only government acquisition of private property triggers the requirement of payment of just compensation under the Fifth Amendment. However, takings jurisprudence also applies when government regulation adversely affects a private property owner's interest in his property. Courts look to the character of the invasion and its economic effect. Here the character of the invasion is not physical; there is no permanent occupation of Norris's land. Absent a permanent physical occupation, compensation is required only if the landowner's primary economic expectations have been thwarted. He will argue that he intended to build on the site for $50 million, and now he must pay $60 million. Thus his expectations have been thwarted to the tune of $10 million. The city will argue that the increase in cost does not thwart legitimate expectations; business people must always factor in cost increases. He intended to build an apartment, and he may do so. The additional costs can be passed along to the tenants. With similar logic the court will also deny Norris's request for additional funds paid to the architect.

III. Norris v. City: Damages during moratorium

The city need not pay lost profits during the moratorium. Norris will argue that during the moratorium (five years), his property was rendered valueless, and therefore the *Lucas* test must apply, requiring compensation. Norris will argue that takings jurisprudence always requires just compensation when land is rendered valueless. He is incorrect. In the first place this is just the kind of regulation that was substance of common law nuisance, taking the case out of the ambit of *Lucas*. Second, *Tahoe* specifically sanctioned moratoria to allow further study of environmental risk. The city will argue that the moratorium lasted a reasonable amount of time to allow it to redraft its ordinance. Takings jurisprudence does not allow a landowner to focus on discrete temporal segments to argue that during some period the land was valueless. Moreover, other uses of the land were permitted during that time, demonstrating that the argument that the land was rendered valueless is without substance.

PROPERTY ESSAY EXAM #3

QUESTION #1

I. Greenie v. Grouchfield

1. Copyright Protection   The list is not subject to copyright protection. Copyright law rewards the creative process of those who produce writings. Greenie will argue that its employee did not aimlessly engage in internet surfing. Rather, Greenie will argue that "Googling" is a skill, like creating poetry or writing prose, and the fruits of it (gathering addresses) ought to be protected. Grouchfield will argue that the creative spark is absent. What was produced was the functional equivalent of a phone book, the compilation of which from public information is not protected.

2. Right of Publicity   The book is protected by Greenie's right to publicity. Greenie will argue that it markets products for profit under its name, and that it therefore exploits its institutional personality. Courts have protected individuals, usually celebrities, who do the same by creating a common law right of publicity. This book has value because Greenie produces it. As such, all attempts to use its name infringes on that right. Grouchfield will argue that the right in common law adhered only to famous individuals, and ought not to extend to institutions, which can defend their intellectual property rights through the traditional categories of copyright, trademark, and patent. Moreover, Greenie cannot claim the common law right because it does not market its persona; rather, it markets its business.

3. Passing Off   Is Grouchfield passing off his book as Greenie's directory? The law does not permit an individual to sell a different product in such a manner so as to suggest it is the same one that is produced by another. Greenie will argue that Grouchfield is misrepresenting the book as the official Greenie directory by creating one very similar, and not making it clear that it is not the official one. This argument Grouchfield will reject; the facts make it clear that he merely is offering a volume for sale, not the official Greenie directory.

4. Unfair Competition   Greenie will argue that it is a competitor of Grouchfield and that Grouchfield has appropriated its work product to produce a similar product to sell to the same customer base as Greenie, which he can do at a lesser price because he is free rider on Greenie's labor. Greenie had to include the expenses of compilation in the price of its directory; Grouchfield did not, so of course he can undercut Greenie's price. Thus the playing field is not level, the essence of unfair competition.

II. Greenie v. Grouchfield

Law of Capture and Finders   Greenie will argue that the law of capture should apply: that the information on alums was similar to a group of wild animals, and that the labor of its employee reduced the information to Greenie's possession. Capture principles have been applied by analogy to property rights other than wild animals, for example, minerals. Greenie will argue that the law of capture protects labor, and that its efforts were central to the accumulation of the information.

In addition, Greenie will resort to the law of finders: the addresses had been in the possession of the institution and were lost. Grouchfield will argue that neither the law of capture nor that of finders should be stretched here. The addresses were neither lost (the institution never had possession of them), nor were they in any sense wild (they were not capable of ownership).

QUESTION #2

I. Zonoroff v. G. W.: Prescription

By 1992, an easement was created by prescription appurtenant to the mine. An easement can be acquired by prescription where the party so asserting proves open, continuous, and exclusive use of a path without permission of the titleholder for the period of the statute of limitations. Zonoroff will argue that its use was not concealed, that it was regular, and that it was not undertaken in conjunction with others. Finally, there was no permission given by G. W. G. W. will argue that he was not in residence and was not aware of the adverse use of the path. This argument will fail: the law requires landowners to monitor the use of their land or suffer the consequences.

II. G. W. v. Zonoroff

1. Termination Through Interference with Use   The fencing-in and locking of the gate was an attempt to terminate the easement that failed. An easement may be terminated when its use and enjoyment is interfered with in an open, continuous, and notorious fashion, without the objection of the holder of the easement. G. W. will argue that the lock was a manifestation of his control over the use of the easement, his intention to turn it into a permissive license. But it was too late. The easement existed, and by giving Zonoroff's employee the key he did not control its use for the prescriptive period that arguably would have terminated it. Zonoroff will argue that it never accepted the act of G. W. as hostile. Merely giving permission to one who already has the right will not transform an easement into a license. The burden is on the landowner to prove permissive use, and G. W. will be unable to do so.

2. Termination Through Abandonment   G. W. will argue that the gating and locking had its desired effect; Zonoroff no longer used the easement. Thus the easement was also terminated by abandonment. Zonoroff will argue that lack of use was not abandonment; it retained the key, and planned to use it when it was convenient. This argument should prevail, because courts are reluctant to find that individuals voluntarily relinquish valuable property.

III. G. W. v. Zonoroff: Termination by exceeding scope of easement

The installation of the wires was beyond the scope of the easement and a timely objection by G. W. may require removal or a forced sale of the right. By stringing wires over poles, Zonoroff has gone beyond the scope of the easement acquired by prescription. G. W. will argue that this improper use of the easement should terminate the right of way. Zonoroff will argue that the offending use creates no greater burden to the land and is therefore within the right of way acquired. However, even if it is not, the entire easement ought not to be terminated, because the improper use (wires) may be separated from the proper use (pathway). Zonoroff may argue that an easement for the wires was created by estoppel. The poles and wires were erected under G. W.'s eyes, and he did not protest. Having had the opportunity to complain and having failed to do so, he is now estopped from objecting. Zonoroff's uncontested activity (a license) occasioned expenditure in reliance; the license is irrevocable. If any compensation ought to be forthcoming, its measure ought to be the decrease in the fair market value of G. W.'s property; that is, his loss.

IV. G. W. v. Zonoroff: Obligation to repair easement

Zonoroff will argue that the law requires that the holder of servient interest (the land subject to the easement) maintain the easement. The road was cut through G. W.'s land; therefore he should be obligated to maintain it. Because he has failed to repair, Zonoroff will argue that he had no alternative but to repair, and he ought to be able to charge the costs to G. W.'s account. G. W. will argue that most courts permit the holder of the easement to enter the servient estate to repair, a so-called secondary easement. Having exercised the secondary easement by repairing the road, G. W. will argue that courts should require the party who derives most benefit from the easement to pay the cost. Since Zonoroff uses the road far more frequently than G. W., the former should pay the cost of repair. Most courts would support G. W.'s position.

V. G. W. v. Zonoroff: Termination and damages for overuse

The excessive use of the easement may be enjoined. G. W. will argue that when the easement was acquired by prescription, the use was more modest than it now is. Overuse terminates an easement. Zonoroff will argue that easements may be used consistent with that quantum agreed by the parties. Since this easement was created by prescription, there was no fixed amount of use contemplated by the parties. Therefore, Zonoroff may make reasonable use. Reasonable use allows increase in the amount of use made at the time of creation. The court should make a determination of a baseline of reasonable use, and allow G. W. to regulate Zonoroff's use consistent therewith. In addition, G. W. should be awarded for pecuniary losses occasioned by the overuse.

QUESTION #3

I. Norris v. Corps

1. Exercise of Police Powers   Norris will claim that the project is not a valid exercise of the police power because it does not protect the public from harm. Rather it confers a benefit on private landowners at his expense. The Army will claim that such projects do benefit the public in general because they reduce flooding on public land as well, and facilitate the provision of public services in flood-prone areas. The Army will argue that it operates pursuant to legislative authority, which is given great deference by courts. The plan by the Army Corps is a valid exercise of the police power.

2. Fifth Amendment Taking   Norris will argue that the flooding of his land is a taking. When government conduct requires an individual property owner to suffer a physical invasion, the right to exclude has been taken. Compensation is always required when the invasion is permanent, and here it is arguable whether the water will recede. The Army will argue that the physical invasion is not by individuals, but by water, a natural resource. Compensation is ordered only when entry by an individual is directed. Norris should prevail on that issue, because government conduct is the direct cause of the invasion, and is knowingly undertaken. However, the Army will argue that the water will recede, leaving Norris with his land augmented. That confers upon him a reciprocity of advantage, which mitigates a takings claim. However, whether the land will return is a fact issue, and should be addressed with that of just compensation, rather than liability for a taking.

Norris will also argue that a segment of his land is valueless and he should therefore be compensated for it under *Lucas*. The court will find that he may not regard his property as discrete segments. Much of his land is still usable for the purposes for which it was used prior to the government's act, so there is no thwarting of his primary expectations for the land. The diminution in value is modest.

II. Norris v. Corps: Just compensation

Compensation should be limited because the taking is temporary, and there may be some reciprocity of advantage of the project to Norris and his property. Assuming a taking, Norris must receive just compensation for the property acquired by the government. Norris will argue that the taking decreased his profits. The Army will argue that lost profits are rarely awarded in takings cases. The Army did not acquire his business. The Army will argue that the proper measure of damages is the decreased value of his land: the difference between the fair market value of the property before and after the governmental act. Moreover, the Army will argue that the taking is temporary, and also that Norris's land will eventually increase in quantity. This latter fact gives him reciprocity of advantage that ought to be regarded as a set-off to his claim. Since the loss in value will be potentially for fewer years than the years of gain, minimal or token compensation is warranted. As to the factual issue of whether the water will recede, the court should make Norris await the eventual outcome of the project before conceding more than token compensation.

PROPERTY ESSAY EXAM #4

QUESTION #1

I. Due v. Shermanfork and Coward: Trespasser or innocent improver?

Due will argue that while he was trespassing on Shermanfork's land, he was in peaceful possession. His occupation was neither violent nor criminal. He ought to be regarded much like an innocent improver. He should receive the value of his labor discounted by some calculation of reasonable rent. Returning the cabin and land to Shermanfork gives the latter a windfall. Moreover, the logs were cut down and abandoned, and Due found them, giving him a greater right than anyone including the true owner, because the true owner had abandoned them. The true owner did not conduct a diligent search for the property.

Shermanfork will argue that the innocent improver doctrine should not apply to those who know that the land is not theirs. Due is a mere squatter who is accorded no profit of the land owing to his own labor. A trespasser upon land cannot acquire rights in property found on the land. Besides, the logs were never lost; Shermanfork had constructive possession of all the personal property on his land. There was no intention on his part to abandon the logs; indeed he did not even know of them.

Likewise Coward will argue that as true owner he has a greater right than Due, who was a mere finder. Coward never intended to abandon his property; it just went down the wrong stream.

II. Shermanfork v. Due and Coward: The landowner

Shermanfork will argue that as the owner of the locus, he had the right to cut down the trees. While he did license Coward to enter his land and cut down trees, the latter abandoned them in the stream. The logs should be regarded as mislaid, purposely left, and forgotten by Coward.

Shermanfork will argue that Coward cannot prove his lumberjacks chopped down the trees. Due may have chopped down the trees, and Sherman will argue that the agreement allows Coward and not trespassers to log, and unless he can prove that his men cut down the logs it should be presumed Due did, unlawfully, and therefore the logs are the property of the landowner. Due cannot be Coward's agent; Coward was not even aware of his conduct. There can be no implied agency; no agreement, no agency. Shermanfork seems likely to get a windfall.

III. Coward v. Shermanfork and Due: Licensee

Coward seems to have had a license to enter Shermanfork's land and cut down the trees. Whether Coward receives the value of the logs or the house depends on whether the court finds that he abandoned the logs. Coward will argue that since he had purchased the right to fell timber on Shermanfork's land, the logs must be his property. Given the lease, he will argue that so long as the logs are likely to have come from the land under lease, a question of fact, the logs should be his property. Shermanfork will argue that Coward cannot prove his lumberjacks chopped down the trees, and unless he can prove that his men cut down the logs it should be presumed that others did, unlawfully, and therefore the logs are the property of the landowner.

QUESTION #2

I. Taking

1. Exercise of Police Power   Wall will question the validity of the Act. He will argue that the provision of low-income housing is a not a valid exercise of the police power: in what way is harm to the public avoided? What the Act does is require him to use his land for the benefit of the public. The Act allows the city to satisfy its obligation, to provide low-income housing, at Wall's expense rather than at its own expense. If the city requires a low-income housing project, let it build one. The city will argue that there has been no physical invasion of the property. The zoning regulation in question merely regulates land use. Wall can continue to use the property in the manner that it has been used before the fire. Moreover, the Act provides administrative review in situations in which a variance from its terms is sought. The Low-Income Housing Act is a valid exercise of the police power.

2. Fifth Amendment Taking   Even though it is a valid exercise of the police power, the zoning ordinance may be a taking as applied to Wall's property. Wall will argue that his primary investment-backed expectations for his property have been thwarted. He seeks to undertake an otherwise lawful project that will enhance the value of the land and also benefit the community. Although the premises had been used as low-income housing before the fire, investment-backed expectations should not be frozen in time. His intentions have always been to derive as much return as possible from his land.

The city will respond by noting that his primary intention was to use the property as a low-priced hotel, and he can continue to do so. He is still left with a profitable use of land, and he has alternatives that may be even more profitable. He is free to combine housing/non-housing use; and he can also build his cinemas on his land, if he builds low-income housing elsewhere.

Penn Central analysis is most appropriate. There is not "trespass, and significant diminution in value from that use to which the property has long been put." The city's argument is probably sufficient to prevail.

3. Board's Abuse of Discretion   The city planning board may have abused its discretion by failing to approve the variance. Wall will argue that the fire destroyed the property, and repairs would be costly; therefore, he is within the exception of subsection (a). Moreover, the expense of rebuilding would be regarded as excessive when compared to the potential return. Thus subsection (c) also applies.

The planning board's discretion is limited to fact-finding, and the facts asserted by Wall clearly meet the legislative mandate. The city will argue that the ordinance states a general prohibition followed by exceptions. The planning board's role is not limited to fact-finding. The board has the discretion to determine whether a variance was in order, subject to a general requirement that its decision be made in good faith. Wall's application for a variance was considered and denied.

4. Unconstitutional Conditions   The city will argue that the regulation has a clause within it that allows development of housing with commercial rents so long as Wall builds a low-income alternative. This is rather like *Nollan* and *Dolan,* where the building of a development was conditioned upon undertaking some act (conveying some property interest to the public) with respect to the property to compensate the public for the harm occasioned by the development, but was in fact unrelated to the development. Wall will argue that this analysis applies to the facts here because the fire, not his development, caused the decline in the quantity of low-income housing units. The project itself has no effect on the number of low-income units. He is not tearing them down to build, merely building on what is unoccupied land. He should prevail.

II. Measure of damages

Should the court find a taking, the measure of damages should be the difference between the fair market value as unregulated land (the value of the building lot as a potential cinema complex) and the fair market value as regulated (the hotel). Wall will argue that the measure of damages should be his pecuniary loss; lost profits over the time the cinema would operate. The city will argue that a cinema has not been acquired. A use has been curtailed. The measure of damages should be the decreased use value: the difference between the fair market value as unregulated land (the value of the building lot as a potential cinema complex) and the fair market value as regulated (the hotel).

QUESTION #3

I. Jasepea v. Landlord

1. Implied Warranty of Suitability   Jasepea will argue that the landlord knew that he was planning on using the property for a restaurant and that parking was essential. Since the parking lot was common property controlled by the landlord, it was clear that the lease implied a promise to plow. The implied warranty of suitability requires him to show that, due to the landlord's default, the premises cannot be used for the intended commercial purpose. It is the commercial equivalent of the implied warranty of habitability in that the tenant may remain and pay reduced rent. Advising Jasepea to move out on the implied warranty of suitability theory is dangerous because if he does and the court finds for the landlord (as it is likely to do), Jasepea is liable for the rest of the lease period.

2. Constructive Eviction: Covenant of Quiet Enjoyment   Jasepea might argue that the landlord breached the covenant of quiet enjoyment. This breach of duty should allow him to claim a constructive eviction, because he gave the landlord notice and he quit the premises. Though usually construed to include prohibitions against affirmative acts by the landlord that interfere with the tenant's use and enjoyment, it has also been found to include failure to act when there is a duty to act. Thus the failure to plow could be a breach of Jasepea's quiet enjoyment. The landlord will argue that the leasehold is still suitable for commercial use; the failure to plow is a minor dereliction, which does not justify damages, no less a termination of the lease. Likewise, the landlord will argue that even if affirmative duties are implied within the covenant, Jasepea has given inadequate notice of breach. A more appropriate remedy would be "repair and deduct": get a person to plow and deduct cost from the rent. But advising Jasepea to move out on the constructive eviction theory is dangerous, because if he does and the court finds for the landlord (as it is likely to do), Jasepea is liable for the rest of the lease period.

II. Beatrice v. Jasepea: Landlord tort liability

Jasepea may be able to pass along tort damages should Beatrice sue and prevail. Landlords are not usually liable for torts that occur on demised premises. An exception is recognized for those that occur on property that the lessees enjoy in common. This seems to be the case here. The landlord will argue that Wall and her customers assumed the risk of slippery walks, and that Jasepea should have "repaired and deducted" — had someone shovel and charge the cost against the rent.

QUESTION #4

I. Norris v. Jesse: Adverse possession

Norris may have acquired the five-foot strip by adverse possession. Norris will argue that for the limitation period of five years (according to the statute provided), he used the land in an open, continuous, exclusive, and adverse manner. He did not conceal his use; the use was uninterrupted by anyone, including the titleholder; he did not use it in concert with others, and he claimed it as his right. Jesse will argue that Norris was mistaken as to ownership, and was therefore not adverse. In some jurisdictions, only land that the adverse possessor knows is not his or her own can be adversely possessed. But other jurisdictions do not draw that distinction, finding adversity in the acts of possession or requiring "good faith" occupation. Under these two formulations of adverse possession Norris will prevail.

Innocent Improver Doctrine Regardless of whether he prevails on adverse possession, and even if he does, Norris can argue that he was an innocent improver; he believed the land was his and should retain the right to possess it, since he invested money to make it satisfy his needs. Jesse will argue that there was no innocence, that Norris knew he was using the land of another, and the doctrine should not be applied. Even if the doctrine is applied, Jesse will argue that he deserves to be paid. He should receive under this theory the decrease in value of his property should the court find that he must grant the five-foot strip of land to Norris.

II. Norris v. Jesse: Covenant running with the land

The writing executed between Norris and Sal created a real covenant, the burden of which runs with the land to the current titleholder, Jesse. Real covenants are interests in property that may require an owner to do an act or refrain from doing an act on property for the benefit of another property owner. Here Jesse is asked to keep the ditch clean. Norris will argue that the requirements of a real covenant were satisfied. First, there was intent that the covenant run with the land because the writing mentions the heirs and assigns of Sal (which Jesse is). Second, the agreement was between those in horizontal privity because the two owners (Sal and Norris) already had existing covenants — clause 2,345,678 — respecting their property. Third, Sal and Jesse are in vertical privity, because Sal transferred his property to Jesse (Jesse's title search would have revealed the agreement because it was "recorded"). Finally, the agreement "touched and concerned" the land, because it conferred a benefit on the land (indeed a mutual benefit).

Jesse will argue that the promise is personal between Norris and Sal and it does not bind him. Jesse's only argument is that there was not intent for the promise to run; heirs and assigns is mere boilerplate, and had Sal expected Jesse to be burdened he would have placed it in the deed of transfer of the land from himself to Jesse.

III. Jesse v. Norris: Covenant running with the land

There is another covenant running with the land. Jesse will claim that the clause limiting building to within five feet of walls created a real covenant. All of the requirements set out above are present with respect to this covenant. Norris will claim intent to run is not specifically mentioned and therefore binds only purchasers from the developers. Moreover, he will argue that the benefit (the power to enforce) does not run to successors in the development like Jesse. Finally, Norris will argue that the appropriate measure of damages should be monetary damages, and that they are minimal. The alternative of removal would be too costly. Moreover, owners have acquiesced to the beams. An injunction ordering removal should be barred though laches.

IV. Jesse v. Norris: Nuisance

Jesse may seek removal of the beams in an action in nuisance. For Jesse to prevail in nuisance under the Restatement requires him to prove that there is an intentional and unreasonable invasion. The invasion issue is a serious one for Jesse because there is no intrusion, physical or metaphysical. Unsightliness? What sort of interference? With a negative easement of view? Let's assume it is done knowingly and so it is within the Restatement's broad view of intentional conduct. But is it unreasonable? Norris is the actor, so we focus on the social utility of his conduct, and balance it with the gravity of the harm to Jesse. With an amenity versus a mudslide, Norris's loss is greater. Besides, should the injunction be issued ordering Norris to tear down the fruits of a significant investment?

The other nuisance formulation, for example, that the burden is serious (difficult to prove) and Norris can afford to pay its costs, is more suited to situations in which the invasion is caused by a commercial enterprise. Besides, what are Jesse's damages — has his property value been decreased?

The common law is just as difficult for Jesse. Norris's beams were constructed before Jesse's purchase; they are "first in time, first in right." Moreover, Norris is fighting a "common enemy." There seems to be no element of spite in his conduct.

PROPERTY ESSAY EXAM #5

QUESTION #1

I. Grouchfield

Grouchfield will argue that he found abandoned property, the script, and has rights as against all other claimants. A finder of property, here Grouchfield, has rights in found property against all persons except the true owner. He will argue that Wall, the author, and arguably the owner, sold the book to Remark, and thereby transferred his right: he manifested an intention to part with his right. Likewise, that Wall never tried to reclaim or use the script is evidence that his sale of the book constituted an abandonment of the script. Grouchfield will argue that he brought this discarded property back into the stream of commerce, and should be rewarded by receiving the profits from its exploitation.

II. Remark

Remark will argue that Grouchfield was an invitee on his premises, but for a limited purpose; he was not invited to find or appropriate any property on the premises. Moreover, he will argue that since he purchased the book, it was under his care in the house, in his constructive possession. Thus it was never lost, and could not be found. The purchase of the book included the purchase of the writing inside. To allow Grouchfield to reap the profits of exploitation would encourage guests to hunt for windfalls in the property of their hosts.

III. Wall

Wall will argue that copyright law protects the writings of authors. Should he be able to substantiate his authorship, he would claim that the creative spark is his rather than Grouchfield's and his failure to register his right should not prejudice his right. His labor produced the script. Copyright in written work extends at least as long as his life. The fact that he did not choose to exploit it until now does not constitute an abandonment of his right. He must, however, somehow argue that he retained some copy of the work for prospective future exploitation. Authors are artists, and may sometimes act eccentrically; that conduct ought not to be regarded as a waiver of his rights.

QUESTION #2

I. Takings: Maseratti v. City

Validity of Ordinance   The zoning ordinance may be challenged as an invalid exercise of the police power. Zoning ordinances are presumed valid, but must be enacted by the government pursuant to the police power, the obligation on the part of the government to protect the public from harm. The city would argue that courts generally review zoning that affects Fifth Amendment property rights with loose scrutiny. A reasonable legislature could determine that eyesores harm the economic value of everyone's land. They do not need under this standard of review to actually demonstrate the decreased value.

Jasepea will challenge the ordinance as an invalid exercise of the police power. He will question whether harm to the public is created by the building of the tower. At most there might be increased traffic from curiosity seekers. The facts suggest spot zoning — that it was directed at a specific plot of land, or that the governmental act was made in bad faith, for a particular, private rather than public motive. Therefore, it is invalid, unenforceable, and Jasepea will prevail in obtaining an injunction preventing the application of the zoning ordinance to his tower

II. City v. Maseratti

Equitable Servitude   The city council, on behalf of the landowners, will argue that the restriction created an equitable servitude. Equitable servitudes are use restrictions that bind successive landowners. The holder would have to show intent to run and notice, plus, in some jurisdictions, touch and concern. The city council would argue that the promise between Luciano and the developer runs with the land because, though not expressly stated in the restriction, the intent to bind successors could be inferred. Residential restrictions only make sense if successor owners are subject to the covenant. They also must touch and concern the land; they must create some economic benefit. Residential restrictions meet that test.

Did Maseratti have notice of the servitude? The city will argue that a title search would have revealed the restriction, and the residential character should have made him realize that there might be restrictions on building. Jasepea will argue that he had no notice of any restrictions when he bought the property in question. A successor must have notice of the burden of an equitable servitude for it to run with the land. While the restriction is not in his deed, the residential character should have put him on notice; he should have looked more carefully at the recorded deeds in his chain of title.

Jasepea will argue that the clause was personal, a promise between Luciano and the developer, and not one that binds successive owners. He will argue that there are no words suggesting that the restriction binds others; for example, "heirs and assigns" does not appear. Moreover, he will argue that the restrictions are too vague to be enforced. There is no way of knowing whether or not his tower will affect the "residential character," or adversely impact property values; some may prefer to live in proximity to the tower, and pay for the privilege. Generally, equitable servitudes must also touch and concern the land. Some economic benefit must accrue to the benefited and burdened lands. As applied to this case, none is apparent. Considering all of these arguments, it is a close call dependent on whether the court finds the tower to be out of character in a residential neighborhood.

Jasepea will argue that the residents have delayed in seeking a remedy, and the injunction should be denied. He has already made an investment, which would be lost. Damages should be the appropriate remedy, if the neighbors prove a loss in the value of their property. The neighbors will argue that they pursued their remedy expeditiously. The case requires a judgment call on the part of the court.

QUESTION #3

I. Norris v. Stout

Common Law Nuisance and the Restatement The floodlight may be a nuisance at common law or under the Restatement §§821 et seq. A nuisance occurs when there is a non-trespassory intentional invasion caused by one individual into the property of another, which is unreasonable. Here the light can be regarded as an invasion, and it is intentional because Stout, though he may not act for the purpose of having the light shine on Norris's land, knows that the light illuminates the rear of the house. Is it unreasonable? For an injunction the plaintiff must show that the gravity of the harm to him outweighs the social utility to the actor. The toughest question for Norris is whether the harm is grave — sleep loss is serious, but certainly the birds could be moved at night so they would be silent. That would also deal with the breeding issue. On the other hand, it is easy to avoid; perhaps Stout ought to be ordered to move his floodlight; the light need not shine in a particular place to discourage burglars; motion detectors could be installed. Since the burden is on Norris to prove that on balance the conduct's harm outweighs its utility, he may not be able to meet the standard. In short, Norris has other options. The Restatement also has another formulation for unreasonable behavior: when the harm is serious, but the actor can afford to compensate the injured party without having to forgo the use. Here the harm doesn't appear serious, but still Stout can buy heavier curtains for Norris.

The common law formulation looks to whether the actor's use is noxious. Here it is not. Nor is a spite fence, another situation which makes the actor's conduct actionable. There is no suggestion of malice. Finally, the common law looked to which conduct was first in time; it was considered first in right. It is not clear whether the floodlight or the situation with the birds was first in time.

II. Norris v. Stout

Easement by Prescription Stout may have created an easement in Norris's land by prescription. Open, notorious, continuous, exclusive, non–permissive use may give rise to an easement by prescription to have light pass over onto Norris's land. The statutory period of ten years has been satisfied. The issue of open and notorious use is tough. Norris may argue that a ray of light is not sufficient to place an individual on notice that an interest in his property is being acquired. Was it continuous? It was only at night. But that shouldn't matter because security lights are generally used at night. Was it adverse? Norris may be able to argue he permitted it, and therefore it was not adverse, so long as there was no inconvenience. Now that there is a conflict, he objected in a timely fashion. The statute of limitations does not run during the permissive period.

QUESTION #4

I. Sherman v. Greenie

1. Deviation from Express Use Limitation Courts generally allow deviations from express provisions under a lease for commercial frustration. But that requires circumstances that were unforeseeable at the time the lease was executed. Sherman will argue that he should be permitted to deviate from the express terms of the lease on the theory of commercial frustration. He will concede that while he agreed to the limitation, it was prior to the health warnings on bagels. He must demonstrate that something beyond his control has effectively rendered the lease commercially impractical. In light of the warnings, nobody will eat bagels; therefore, the purpose of the lease, to sell coffee with bagels, has been frustrated commercially. Moreover, he will argue that it is unreasonable to apply the literal terms of the lease, because the expansion does not affect the landlord's retained property; the addition of croissants does not seem to affect other lessees' businesses, or the operation of the university. Likewise the tutoring seems to have no undesirable effect on other property and their values. The case would be different if this was a shopping center and a commercial landlord was apportioning uses among tenants. Greenie will argue that the law permits tenants and landlords to bargain for restrictions on use in leases. Here the parties limited Sherman's use to only one form of bread, bagels, and that the court should enforce literally the provision.

2. Constructive Eviction   Even if the court does not find commercial frustration, it may be possible for Sherman to rescind the lease and quit the premises claiming a constructive eviction. Sherman will argue that the interference with the deliveries is a constructive eviction allowing Sherman to quit and terminate the lease. He will argue that the lease has implied warranty of quiet enjoyment: that the landlord covenants not to undertake acts that interfere with the tenant's use and enjoyment of the premises. Blocking deliveries is just such an act, and it is a substantial interference. All he must do is give notice to the landlord that he intends to vacate because of the landlord's breach. Then prior to suit, he must quit. If his claim prevails, he will be absolved of the rent, and may claim relocation costs and any additional rent he would have to pay to secure an alternative venue for his business.

The landlord will argue that the blockade is not a physical interference with the use and enjoyment of the premises. The landlord's act occurs outside of the actual leasehold property. Moreover, the landlord will claim that her conduct is undertaken to enforce a legal obligation that Sherman voluntarily undertook. If Greenie prevails, Sherman will be liable for rent for the rest of the leasehold term, though the landlord may have an obligation to hold the premises open for a replacement tenant.

The court will probably sustain Sherman's claim. Constructive eviction has been expanded as a tenant's remedy to include actions by the landlord outside of the confines of the premises, and even extended to the acts of the landlord's other tenants. The landlord's conduct seems to be a heavy-handed attempt to enforce the terms of an agreement that ought to be settled by negotiation or litigation.

II. Sherman v. Greenie: Injunction

If Sherman wishes to continue his business on the leasehold premises, he ought to be able to enjoin the blockade on the grounds that a deviation in the lease terms should be permitted on the commercial frustration theory. Sherman will argue that he should be permitted to deviate from the express terms of the lease on the theory of commercial frustration. He will concede that while he agreed to the limitation, it was prior to the health warnings on bagels. He must demonstrate that something beyond his control has effectively rendered the lease commercially impractical. In light of the warnings, nobody will eat bagels; therefore, the purpose of the lease, to sell coffee with bagels, has been frustrated commercially. Moreover, he will argue that it is unreasonable to apply the literal terms of the lease, because the expansion does not affect the landlord's retained property; the addition of croissants does not seem to affect other lessees' businesses, or the operation of the university. Likewise the tutoring seems to have no undesirable effect on other property and their values. The case would be different if this was a shopping center and a commercial landlord was apportioning use among tenants.

PROPERTY ESSAY EXAM #6

QUESTION #1

I. Uchello v. Air Force

The cases raises two separate issues: is the use by the Air Force a nuisance; or is it a taking?

1. Nuisance   Uchello has three separate nuisance claims: that the AF has contaminated his groundwater; that the near overflights create "noise pollution"; and that the toilets are an odorous eyesore. Let's examine each claim under the common law of nuisance, and Restatement §§821 et seq.

a. The Groundwater   Under the common law, Uchello will argue that the conduct of the AF is a "noxious use." Traditional law makes value judgments on the actor's (here AF) conduct. The chemical that is seeping into the groundwater is toxic and therefore intrinsically harmful. It is a "physical invasion" of Uchello's land by chemicals owned and used under the control of the AF. The AF can make a weak argument that it arrived first in time (that is, it operated the airfield before Uchello bred cattle) and therefore ought to be able to continue its actions. That argument ought to be disregarded because the chemical is dangerous, and its presence seems to preclude almost any lawful use by Uchello of his ranch.

Under the Restatement, Uchello must show that there is an invasion of his property occasioned by acts of the AF and that the invasion is intentional and unreasonable. Intentional does not mean purposeful (that the result is desired by the AF); "knowingly" is sufficient — that the AF understood that its conduct would result in the invasion. That is clear from the facts. But Uchello must prove that the AF's conduct was "unreasonable." In seeking to enjoin the actor's conduct, the party claiming that the act is the nuisance (Uchello) must show that the gravity of the harm to him outweighs its overall social utility. The AF may argue national defense. But the court may look to the factor set out in §828(c) — that resultant seepage could be avoided. Uchello will argue that the gravity of the harm is great, and that his use of the land has economic value and is well suited to the area. Should the court accept the AF's national security argument, Uchello could argue he should be compensated under §826(b). The harm is great, and the AF can compensate him for his loss: the dead cattle and the value of the land that can no longer be used.

b. Noise Pollution   A tougher row to hoe. Under the common law, excessive noise has not been generally regarded as a nuisance. Is it really an "invasion"? Nuisances can result from non-trespassory invasions. The AF's use of land adjacent to Uchello's as a staging area is not per se noxious. Thus a first in time argument by the AF might be more persuasive.

Under the Restatement, Uchello must show an intentional and unreasonable invasion. The fact that noise is not a physical intrusion is not relevant: the invasion can be non-trespassory. The same "intentional" argument as above can be lodged. But is it unreasonable: does the gravity of the harm outweigh the social utility of the AF's conduct? Here the extent of the harm to Uchello is much less. The AF will claim that defense is important to society. On the other hand, could the noise not easily be abated?

    c. The "Johnnys"   Under the common law, an even tougher row to hoe. Two complaints are lodged here: the view and the odor. As to the view, where's the invasion? Uchello's sensibilities are affected by the view. On the other hand, Uchello might argue that the odor is a factor, though he seems to have discounted it. Creation of odors did give rise to nuisances at common law: the proverbial pig in the parlor. And he was first in time. Moreover, Groberts seems to be acting with malice. It seems to be a "spite fence."

    Under the Restatement, Uchello must show an intentional and unreasonable invasion. The visual impairment does not seem like an invasion, either trespassory or non-trespassory. Since it is difficult to see the invasion, it is not easy to determine whether it is "intentional." Certainly the AF is aware that Uchello regards the conduct as unpleasant so the AF's conduct is knowing. Gravity of the harm versus social utility? The harm seems minor, but it would be easy for the AF to avoid it. While the odor is more like an invasion (of smelly air), and it is "intentional" in that the AF is aware of its conduct, the gravity of the harm versus social utility of the conduct is a close call. Uchello's best argument is that it is easy for the AF to avoid the invasion by moving the johns.

    Oddly then, in the last cause of action for nuisance, the johns, Uchello is more like to prevail under "old" nuisance law than under the "modern" formulation of the Restatement.

II. Uchello v. AF: Takings

    Uchello could argue that the AF has "taken" his land and would therefore be required under the Fifth Amendment to pay just compensation. He would argue that the pollution constitutes a permanent physical trespass, and in such cases the government must always pay just compensation, here the difference in value between his spread before and after the pollution. The government could purchase the polluted areas. Even if the court rejects the "taking by trespass" argument, because the trespass if any is below ground (which it shouldn't because land ownership extends from the surface upward to the heavens and downward to the nether world), he can maintain that his primary expectations for the land have been thwarted, and that the value of his land has been diminished and he has received no reciprocity of advantage from the AF's acts. The case falls squarely within *Penn Central*.

> ## QUESTION #2

I. Benenatti v. City/Law School

    Two interests may have been created: an easement by prescription; and some part of the lot by adverse possession.

1. Adverse Possession   Benenatti will argue that she has acquired ownership of the lands occupied through adverse possession. She will argue that she was in actual possession of the area around her WV (the WV was parked on the lot and she used the area around the WV for regular parties). Her use was open and notorious; it was not done surreptitiously, so a reasonably vigilant titleholder would be aware of her occupation. It was continuous because the WV was there except when she drove it to church. It was used regularly — not all the time, but for discrete periods, as the titleholder of a vacant lot might use such land. It was exclusive. Those who entered were invitees; and the titleholder never used the land during the period. An issue is adversity or hostility. Benenatti will argue that she met the requirements of both the Maine rule (she knew the land was not hers, but she claimed the right to use it regardless) and the Connecticut rule (state of mind of the adverse possessor is assumed from the act of occupation). The statute only requires 20 years of occupation, and she has been there nearly twice as long. Forty years of adverse possession probably meets any state's time limitation.

The city/law school will claim that her acts of actual possession were limited. She was on the property only sporadically. Because the occupation was random, a reasonable vigilant titleholder would not have understood that there was an occupier. That argument will likely fail, because the facts state that the car was parked there daily. The city/law school might say that parking an old car on a vacant lot was insufficiently open and notorious use; a reasonably vigilant titleholder would not have assumed that the wreck was there to stake some sort of lasting claim to any part of the lot. The city/law school would probably concede that Benenatti's use was exclusive, since city employees or indeed others did not seem to enter without Benenatti's permission. The city/law school might object to the continuity of her possession; she was not there all the time. That is a weak argument because owners of land are not always in occupation. The city will argue that Benenatti was not adverse. They will argue that courts are moving to a good faith standard of adversity. The city will note that some jurisdictions require that the occupier have a good faith belief that the property is hers. If the court moves in that direction, Benenatti will lose, but the good faith belief rule is adhered to only in a minority of jurisdictions. The city will also maintain that her use was not adverse because the city had no present use for the land, so her use did not in any way impinge on its own plans. That should not prevent Benenatti from perfecting adverse possession. They would need to show that they licensed Benenatti's use, which does not appear to be the case under the facts.

2. Easement by Prescription   Benenatti could argue that she has an easement by prescription to continue to walk across the part of the lot that she has used to park her Harley. The requirements of an easement by prescription are similar to those for adverse possession, but are expressed in somewhat different terms given the interest to be acquired. Thus, actual possession need not be shown, because, after all, an easement is a non-possessory interest in property. Benenatti must show that she uses a similar path openly and notoriously, again not concealed so a reasonably vigilant owner would notice her use. Continuous does not mean continuous (the holder of an easement by grant is not always using the easement). Rather, it means with sufficient regularity. Exclusive means exclusive of other users, which seems to be the case here. Adversity in prescriptive easement acquisition means that the use was non-permissive. Most courts will require the owner to prove that the use was permissive. There is no evidence that permission was ever granted.

The city's strongest objection to Benenatti's prescription claim is that seasonal use is insufficiently regular to be continuous. She used the path less than half the year. Seasonal use may be sufficient if the type of use is linked to the weather. If crossing a vacant lot in the city is something generally only done from May to September given the climate, use for that period may be sufficient.

II. Actions by Benenatti

Benenatti will bring an action to quiet title against the city. She will claim access to the parking space (perhaps an easement by prescription) and the area around the van. If the city acted first and brought an action in ejectment (to require her to leave), she could use her adverse possession as a defense to the action.

She could bring an action to enjoin any potential interference that the building might bring to her continued use of her easement. It would, however, be reasonable to ask her to use her easement in such a way as to limit impact on the new building.

The city will argue that municipal land is by the statute exempt from adverse possession. The statute lists the governmental entities, federal and state, but does not mention municipalities. Though the city is an emanation of the state, a listing should exclude those governmental entities not included. The city will point to the "nor" clause. They will say it is held for a "public purpose" and as "open spaces." It seems that a vacant car lot is not what the legislature had in mind for "open spaces," and by the time the city set the land to any purpose, Benenatti had been in possession for the period of the limitation.

QUESTION #3

I. Southman/Nash v. Onnig

1. The Nash-Collins Transfer   An equitable servitude may have been created in the transfer of the eastern half of the Nash farmstead to Michael. Southman, who comes into possession of land that was retained by Nash upon the sale of the land to Collins, wants to enforce the restriction. To do so, Southman must hold the benefit of the servitude, and that benefit must run with the land. Likewise, since Onnig owns the land that may be developed, the burden must run with the land.

While Nash was in possession of the land, he could have brought an action against Michael to enjoin the construction based simply on contract law. But since both Michael and Nash have transferred their land, the question is whether the agreement can be enforced against subsequent owners. That raises the issue of whether the initial transfer created an equitable servitude or real covenant.

Equitable servitudes are created when a landowner subjects transferred land to a burden; here that burden is not to impede the view. The transferor and transferee must intend that the burden run with the land, and the successor owner against whom the burden is to be enforced must know that his or her land is burdened.

Onnig will argue that the failure to specifically burden Michael's transferees while giving a cause of action to Nash's transferees is evidence that the street was one way. The benefit ran to Nash's successors, while the burden did not run to Michael's successors. Therefore Onnig does not take subject to the burden. Southman will counter that while Michael doesn't covenant for his "heirs and assigns," intent to bind successor is present because the words "heirs and assigns" are used in the clause when referring to the enforceability: transferor and his heirs and assigns may seek an injunction whenever in the opinion of the transferor and his heirs and assigns the view will be blocked by trees or buildings. Moreover, when Michael resold the lots he limited them to residential use, arguably suggesting that he recognized they were subject to a servitude. But the servitude in the resold land, Michael would argue, is more limited.

The court may find intent because the type of restriction created frequently is intended to bind successors. If it did, the restriction is of limited use: Michael could circumvent it by a transfer to another person or legal entity and thus render the restriction no longer binding. This is particularly the case when an injunction is the remedy. How could one enjoin someone who no longer owns the land? If damages were provided, Southman could claim them and live with the blocked view.

Subsequent purchasers must know of the restriction. Here even though there is no evidence that the restriction is in the deed from Michael to Onnig, a title search would uncover it. Onnig's land is part of the land Nash sold to Michael, and the title searcher should have examined that deed for encumbrances.

Most courts will require that the servitude touch and concern the land, though since this is an equitable servitude and not a real covenant, it may not be required. Still courts will only enforce reasonable restrictions that confer some economic benefit on the land. Both reasonableness and touch and concern are present. The Nash estate is more valuable with a view.

II. No interest was created

At the time the grant is made to Southman, Nash does not own the land he is attempting to burden. If an interest was created in the transfer between Nash and Michael, the issue of whether the benefit runs to Southman is resolved by the analysis above. The fact that Nash believed that there was a benefit may suggest that he intended that the benefits and burdens of the above equitable servitude ran with the land. But his intent alone is insufficient. Michael would also have had to have agreed.

III. An equitable servitude was created

Although it is a close case, an equitable servitude has been created. It is likely that the court will permit Southman to enjoin Onnig from building his condo, because an equitable servitude was created in the transfer between Nash and Michael. The benefit runs to the successors of Nash; the burden runs to the successors of Michael. Onnig might argue that the servitude was terminated when development occurred on the burdened land—the two-story residences, which obscured the view. The fact that the Onnig project is of such a greater magnitude suggests that permitting the earlier modest development, which was arguably not even contrary to the terms of the servitude (the clause in the transfer between Nash and Michael allows Nash to determine what types of development to enjoin), should not bar Southman. But must he get Nash to join in the suit? After all, the clause refers to Nash's judgment.

Can Michael or Nash enjoin Onnig's project? Nash might argue he has a negative easement in gross, a right to the unobstructed view regardless of whether he owns the land or not. However, the wording of the clause does not seem to reserve such a personal right.

QUESTION #4

I. Wall v. City

1. Validity of the Zoning Ordinance   The zoning ordinance is probably a valid exercise of the police power. The community is trying to isolate sex offenders from residing in proximity to children. A rational legislature could believe that the ordinance protects children from potential harm. The Supreme Court in cases like *Belle Terre* allowed zoning ordinances to exclude unrelated individuals from living in houses in areas that are zoned as single family. There is no federally protected right to live where you like. Though the effect is to zone out Wall from the community, there is no showing of bad faith on the part of the council. Wall will argue that to exclude him from the community is rather like the *Shad v. Mount Ephraim* case where the town completely excluded erotic bookstores from the town. Accordingly, Wall might argue that he should not be completely excluded from living in the town. He might argue that there are other ways of protecting children short of excluding him, but in the zoning cases dealing with housing the court merely seeks a rational basis for the ban. Wall might look to state constitutional law, as in *Township of Delta v. Dinolfo* or *NAACP v. Mount Laurel*. Some courts see the right to housing as a stronger constitutional right.

2. A Taking   If the limitation is enforced, Wall might try to argue that the zoning as applied to him is a taking of his property (the defeasible fee) and requires just compensation. Though an imaginative argument, it is not any easy one to substantiate. There is no physical occupation of his land by the government, so the court must find that his investment-backed expectations have been thwarted. The property was a gift, so can he be said to have any investment-backed expectations? On the other hand, this might be a rare case of a situation in which *Lucas* could apply. Compensation is required when property is devalued to zero, and the law does not regulate activity that would be a nuisance at common law. Arguably, he has lost all value in the property. When the government renders land valueless, it must be acting to regulate conduct that would not have been permitted under baseline principles of nuisance at common law. Certainly, his conduct was not.

II. The interest in Wall

The limitation in the grant is a type of defeasible fee simple. Unlike the fee simple determinable or fee simple on a condition subsequent where the possibility of reverter or right of entry is retained by the grantor, this defeasible fee is followed by an executory interest in Flora. Richard might argue that the limitation against remarriage should be regarded as an unenforceable condition, and it is also not the type of "use" limitation that is frequently found in defeasible fee simples. The requirement to reside might be less objectionable, but still the traditional use limitations are, for example, not to use the premises as a bar or a residence.

PROPERTY
MULTIPLE CHOICE
115 QUESTIONS

ANSWER SHEET

Print or copy this answer sheet to all multiple choice questions.

1.	A B C D	30.	A B C D	59.	A B C D	88.	A B C D
2.	A B C D	31.	A B C D	60.	A B C D	89.	A B C D
3.	A B C D	32.	A B C D	61.	A B C D	90.	A B C D
4.	A B C D	33.	A B C D	62.	A B C D	91.	A B C D
5.	A B C D	34.	A B C D	63.	A B C D	92.	A B C D
6.	A B C D	35.	A B C D	64.	A B C D	93.	A B C D
7.	A B C D	36.	A B C D	65.	A B C D	94.	A B C D
8.	A B C D	37.	A B C D	66.	A B C D	95.	A B C D
9.	A B C D	38.	A B C D	67.	A B C D	96.	A B C D
10.	A B C D	39.	A B C D	68.	A B C D	97.	A B C D
11.	A B C D	40.	A B C D	69.	A B C D	98.	A B C D
12.	A B C D	41.	A B C D	70.	A B C D	99.	A B C D
13.	A B C D	42.	A B C D	71.	A B C D	100.	A B C D
14.	A B C D	43.	A B C D	72.	A B C D	101.	A B C D
15.	A B C D	44.	A B C D	73.	A B C D	102.	A B C D
16.	A B C D	45.	A B C D	74.	A B C D	103.	A B C D
17.	A B C D	46.	A B C D	75.	A B C D	104.	A B C D
18.	A B C D	47.	A B C D	76.	A B C D	105.	A B C D
19.	A B C D	48.	A B C D	77.	A B C D	106.	A B C D
20.	A B C D	49.	A B C D	78.	A B C D	107.	A B C D
21.	A B C D	50.	A B C D	79.	A B C D	108.	A B C D
22.	A B C D	51.	A B C D	80.	A B C D	109.	A B C D
23.	A B C D	52.	A B C D	81.	A B C D	110.	A B C D
24.	A B C D	53.	A B C D	82.	A B C D	111.	A B C D
25.	A B C D	54.	A B C D	83.	A B C D	112.	A B C D
26.	A B C D	55.	A B C D	84.	A B C D	113.	A B C D
27.	A B C D	56.	A B C D	85.	A B C D	114.	A B C D
28.	A B C D	57.	A B C D	86.	A B C D	115.	A B C D
29.	A B C D	58.	A B C D	87.	A B C D		

PROPERTY QUESTIONS

Questions 1–4 are based on these facts:

Smith, a second-hand book dealer, purchased a used four-volume set of *Blackstone's Commentaries* from Jones for $200. Jones inherited the book from his Uncle John. Inside the book, he came across a U.S. War Bond made out in the name of Ulysses Wescott, Sergeant, U.S. Army Quartermaster Corps, with a face value of $100. The date of maturity of the bond is January 1, 1970. Even though the bond matured about 40 years ago, the U.S. government continues to be obligated to pay $100. Smith finds out that the value of the bond to collectors is $5,000.

1. How should the property be characterized?

A) Lost.

B) Mislaid.

C) Treasure trove.

D) Abandoned.

2. Before Jones sells the book to Smith, what right does Jones have in the bond?

A) True owner.

B) Possessor.

C) Finder.

D) Bailee.

3. To whom should the bond be awarded?

A) Smith.

B) Jones.

C) Wescott if he is alive; his heirs or devisees if he is not.

D) The U.S. government.

4. Suppose shortly before judgment is entered, Smith sells the bond to Banks for $1,000. Banks is unaware of precisely how Smith came to possess the bond. Assume Wescott has died intestate. Wescott's heirs bring an action against Banks and join Smith.

A) Heirs can collect against Banks and Smith.

B) Heirs can recover against Smith only.

C) Heirs can recover against Banks only.

D) Heirs cannot recover.

Questions 5–7 are based on these facts:

Smith, an amateur photographer who occasionally sells his travel photos to friends who frame them, recently returned from an "around the world in 80 days" cruise. He immediately went to his local camera store to get his dozen rolls of film developed and printed. The clerk gave him a receipt for the film. A week later, Smith returned to the camera store, but the clerk was unable to find the prints, the negatives, or the exposed film.

5. What legal relationship was created between Smith and the camera store?

A) Trust.

B) Bailment.

C) Gift.

D) Conversion.

6. Smith sues the camera store. Which of the following measure of damages can he recover?

A) The value of the film.

B) The value of the photographs.

C) The value of his trip.

D) The cost of a return trip.

7. Suppose the receipt had the following notice in fine print: "Not responsible for lost or damaged film." Which of the following measure of damages can he recover?

A) The value of the film.

B) Sentimental value of the photos.

C) The value of his trip.

D) The cost of a return trip.

8. *Pierson v. Post* involved the application of property law to the appropriation of wild animals. To which of the following circumstances might the law of capture be applied?

A) A baseball hit into the bleachers during a game.

B) Natural gas pumped into an underground cavity that once contained gas.

C) A tame animal returned to the wild.

D) All of the above.

9. Some jurisdictions recognize a common law right of publicity. To whom does this right apply?

A) Anyone.

B) Movie stars.

C) Political figures.

D) Anyone who seeks to market their image for profit.

10. CNN has just reported that an airplane has landed safely on the Hudson River. After hearing the report, Smith dashes to the river to photograph the plane. He sells the photo on the internet. Can CNN seek some share of his profits?

A) Yes, use of the story in this fashion violates its copyright.

B) Yes, Smith's act is an example of unfair competition.

C) No, the scene was "news" and nobody can own the news.

D) No, because by putting out the story, CNN waived all its property right in the story when it aired it.

11. If a student photocopies a page of the library's copy of a treatise on the federal court system from a 300-page treatise, must she compensate the author?

A) Yes, copyright has been violated.

B) Yes, photocopying is a crime.

C) No, the structure of the federal courts is information in the public domain.

D) No, photocopying a page for personal use does not violate copyright.

12. Adverse possession may ultimately have negative implications for society for which of the following reasons?

A) It rewards individuals who use land.

B) It allows those who monitor the lands that they own to avoid a loss of their property right.

C) It discourages owners to allow land to remain undeveloped, and therefore provides some environmental benefit lest another may come, develop the land, and eventually claim title.

D) It encourages litigation.

Questions 13–17 are based on these facts:

In 2004, Jones purchased a five-acre square tract of undeveloped rural land in the frozen north for $10,000 from Smith, who had purchased that land decades ago by quitclaim deed. Jones began to fence off the property. Unbeknownst to either Smith or Jones, Bloggs has used the property each summer since 1983 as a campsite during his month-long vacation. In the spring, Bloggs also taps the maple trees on the land for their sap. Bloggs brings an action to quiet title to the land in 2009. Assume that the state has a 20-year statute of limitations for pursuing rights in land.

13. Which adverse possession requirement has Bloggs arguably not fulfilled by 2003?

A) Actual possession.

B) Open and notorious.

C) Continuous.

D) Exclusive.

14. Suppose in 2000, about 17 years after Bloggs entered onto the land, Jones entered the land while Bloggs was tapping the maple trees. Jones told Bloggs to get off his land, which Bloggs did. Jones then tapped some of the remaining untapped trees. The next day Jones posted "no trespassing" signs. Bloggs returned the following week, and continued his use for the period largely unmolested by Jones, though Jones occasionally tapped the maples in succeeding springs. Has Bloggs fulfilled the requirements for adverse possession?

A) No, Bloggs's entry is no longer adverse.

B) No, Jones's entry is insufficient to interrupt the continuous and exclusive requirement.

C) Yes, Jones's use of the land no longer renders Bloggs's use exclusive.

D) No, Jones's use of the land is minimal, and therefore Bloggs's use remains exclusive.

15. Suppose in 1995 Bloggs died, and willed all his property to his daughter, Bloggs, Jr. Bloggs, Jr. continues to use the property as Bloggs did. In 2003, has the 20-year statute of limitations requirement for adverse possession been fulfilled?

A) No, Bloggs, Jr.'s actual possession has not been for the statutory 20 years.

B) No, Bloggs, Jr. may only tack years if she is in privity of estate with the titleholder.

C) Yes, Bloggs, Jr. inherited the property interest that Bloggs had in the land.

D) Yes, Bloggs, Jr. may tack the years of Bloggs's possession to her own years of possession to achieve the required 20 years of adverse possession.

16. Suppose Jones sold the property in 1995 to White. White does not use or monitor Bloggs's use of the property. In 2009, Bloggs brings an action to quiet title. Will Bloggs prevail?

A) Yes, because Jones and White are in privity, Bloggs can tack the years that Jones owned the property to those that White owned the property.

B) Yes, adverse possession runs against successive owners so long as the underlying requirements are met.

C) No, Jones and White are not in privity.

D) No, Jones and Bloggs are not in privity.

17. Suppose Bloggs believed the property in question was actually owned by his brother during the entire period of his possession. He occupied the property since 1983, as stated in facts. In 2009, Jones brings an action to eject Bloggs from the premises. How should the court resolve the case?

A) Against Bloggs, if the court requires the adverse possessor to act in bad faith under the so-called Maine rule.

B) Against Bloggs, if the court requires the adverse possessor to act in good faith, under the so-called Iowa rule.

C) For Bloggs, if the court does not take into account the subjective state of mind of the adverse possessor under the so-called Connecticut rule.

D) All of the above.

18. Smith holds a life estate in Tanacre. Which of the following acts constitutes waste?

A) He discovers oil on the property and opens up a well.

B) He tears down the residence on the premises.

C) He tears down the residence on the premises and erects a shopping center.

D) All of the above.

19. Smith sells Tanacre to Jones with the following limitation: "so long as the property is not used for the sale of alcoholic beverages, but if alcoholic beverages are sold on the premises the interest in Jones will cease." What interest has been created and/or reserved?

A) Fee simple absolute in Jones.

B) Fee simple determinable in Jones with a possibility of reverter retained by Smith.

C) Fee simple determinable in Jones with a right of entry retained by Smith.

D) Fee simple on a condition subsequent in Jones with a possibility of reverter retained by Smith.

20. Suppose the above limitation states that upon sale of alcoholic beverages the property passes to Smith's godson, Nigel. What interest has been created and/or reserved?

   A) Fee simple subject to an executory interest in Jones, with an executory interest in Nigel.

   B) Fee simple determinable in Jones with a possibility of reverter in Nigel.

   C) Fee simple determinable in Jones with a right of entry retained by Smith that passes to Nigel at Smith's death.

   D) Fee simple on a condition subsequent in Jones with a possibility of reverter retained by Smith that passes to Nigel at Smith's death.

21. At common law, what interest was created when Smith conveyed Tanacre to Jones in the following manner: "to Jones forever"?

   A) A fee simple absolute.

   B) A fee simple determinable.

   C) A life estate.

   D) A fee tail.

22. Under modern interpretation of grants, what interest is probably created when Smith conveyed Tanacre to Jones in the following manner: "to Jones forever"?

   A) A fee simple absolute.

   B) A fee simple determinable.

   C) A life estate.

   D) A fee tail.

23. What future interest is created by the following limitation: "to Smith for life, then if Jones survives Smith to Jones, and her heirs"?

   A) A vested remainder.

   B) An executory interest.

   C) A contingent remainder.

   D) A possibility of reverter.

24. What future interest is created by the following limitation: "to my daughter Prunella when she passes the bar"?

   A) A vested remainder.

   B) A springing executory interest.

C) A contingent remainder.

D) A shifting executory interest.

Questions 25–32 are based on these facts:

Banks conveys Tanacre as follows: "to Smith for life, then to his daughter Amy for life, then to her children and their heirs, but if Jones passes the bar exam during Amy's life then immediately to Jones." Amy has no children alive at the time of the grant.

25. What future interests are created?

A) A vested life estate in remainder in Amy; a contingent remainder in her children in fee simple; an executory interest in Jones.

B) A vested life estate in remainder in Amy; a vested remainder in her children in fee simple; an executory interest in Jones.

C) A vested life estate in remainder in Amy; a vested remainder subject to open and to divestment in her children in fee simple; an executory interest in Jones.

D) A vested life estate in remainder in Amy; a vested remainder subject to open in her children in fee simple; an executory interest in Jones.

26. Smith dies. What impact does that have on the state of the title?

A) Amy's life estate vests.

B) Amy's life estate becomes a present possessory interest.

C) Amy takes Tanacre in fee simple absolute.

D) None of the above.

27. Amy has a child, Bertha. What impact does that have on the state of the title?

A) Amy's life estate terminates.

B) The executory interest in Jones is destroyed.

C) The vested remainder opens to include Bertha.

D) The contingent remainder vests in Bertha subject to open.

28. Jones passes the bar. What impact does that have on the state of the title?

A) Bertha's remainder is divested.

B) Jones takes Tanacre in fee simple absolute.

C) Both A and B.

D) Jones takes Tanacre at the death of Amy.

29. Jones has yet to take the bar. Amy dies. What impact does that have on the state of the title?

A) Bertha takes Tanacre in fee simple absolute.

B) Bertha takes Tanacre until Jones passes the bar.

C) Bertha takes Tanacre for life.

D) All of the above.

30. What if thereafter Jones passes the bar?

A) The possessory estate shifts to Jones in fee simple.

B) The possessory estate remains in Bertha in fee simple.

C) Bertha has a life interest only.

D) None of the above.

31. What if the words "during Amy's life" were not included in the future interest in Jones, and he passes the bar after Amy dies?

A) The same result as above, because the words were implied in the grant.

B) Because Jones's interest is now a contingent remainder, the estate passes to him.

C) If the jurisdiction has not adopted the rules of destructibility of contingent remainders, and does not draw a distinction between executory interest and contingent remainders, the estate would immediately be transferred to Jones.

D) The estate reverts to the grantor because the rule against perpetuities has been violated.

32. Smith conveys Tanacre "to Amy for life, then to Bertha if she reaches the age of 25 for life, then to Carly and her heirs." Bertha is age 20 and Carly is age 18 at the time of the grant. Two years later Carly buys Amy's interest. What are the consequences of the purchase on the title?

A) None, merger occurs only when two vested estates follow each other.

B) The remainder in Bertha is destroyed, and Carly owns Tanacre in fee simple absolute through merger, because she owns a vested life estate and the next succeeding vested interest.

C) The Rule in Shelly's Case creates a fee simple absolute interest in Tanacre in Carly.

D) Under the Doctrine of Worthier Title, Carly owns Tanacre in fee simple absolute.

33. The rule against perpetuities applies to which of the following future interests?

A) Vested remainders.

B) Contingent remainders.

C) Rights of entry.

D) Reversions.

34. Smith conveys Tanacre "to Amy for life, then to Bertha and her heirs when Amy's estate is settled." Does the grant violate the rule against perpetuities? Why or why not?

A) No, both Amy and Bertha are alive at the time of the grant.

B) No, Bertha's interest is vested.

C) Yes, Bertha may die before Amy.

D) Yes, Amy's estate may not be settled within the lifetime of Bertha (or any other life in being) plus 21 years.

Questions 35–39 are based on these facts:

Smith conveys Tanacre "to Amy for life, and then to Amy's widower for life, then to Amy's issue living at the death of the longer lived of Amy and her spouse." Amy is married to Boris at the time of the grant, and has two children, Clare and David.

35. Does the interest in Amy's issue violate the rule against perpetuities?

A) No, the limitation creates only vested interests.

B) No, Boris, Clare, and David are living at the time of the grant.

C) No, although the remainders to the widower and children are contingent, they will vest at the death of Amy, a life in being.

D) Yes, the gifts to the widower and to the children are contingent and one or more may vest outside the period of the rule against perpetuities.

36. How might the scrivener have drafted around the rule?

A) Limit the gift to widower "to Boris."

B) Limit the gift to a "widower born in the lifetime of Amy."

C) Limit the gift to a "widower alive at the time of the grant."

D) A and C.

37. Can a gift be limited to "her widower, with a remainder to her children and their heirs," and not violate the rule against perpetuities?

A) Yes, by limiting the contingent remainder to "her children alive at the time of Amy's death."

B) Yes, by making the remainder contingent upon being alive at the time of the surviving widower's birth.

C) Yes, by making the remainder limited to those living at the time of Amy's death and living at the time for distribution (the death of her widower).

D) A and C.

38. Would the following reforms of the rule against perpetuities likely save the remainder limited to Amy's children?

A) The "wait and see" approach.

B) Cy pres.

C) The Uniform Statutory Rule Against Perpetuities.

D) All of the above.

39. Smith conveys Tanacre "to Amy and her brother Boris and the survivor." What estate is created?

A) A joint tenancy.

B) A tenancy by the entirety.

C) A tenancy in common.

D) Concurrent life estates, with reversion to Smith at the death of the first to die.

Questions 40–43 are based on these facts:

Smith and Jones have been married for five years, and they purchase Tanacre as joint tenants with right of survivorship. They divorce. Smith executes a mortgage on Tanacre in the sum of $40,000 to the Ace Mortgage Company.

40. What effect does the divorce and mortgage have on title to the premises?

A) The divorce has no effect, but the mortgage severs the joint tenancy.

B) Neither the divorce nor the mortgage has an effect on the joint tenancy.

C) The divorce severs the joint tenancy; the mortgage is secured only on Smith's remaining interest.

D) The mortgage is invalid.

41. During the ten years following the divorce, Smith rents out the property. Smith and Jones share the rent, but Smith pays the taxes and maintains the premises. At the end of the tenth year, may Smith bring an action against Jones for half of the expenses?

A) Smith may be reimbursed for taxes, but not for maintenance.

B) Smith may be reimbursed for maintenance, but not for taxes.

C) Smith may be reimbursed for all expenses paid.

D) Smith may be reimbursed for no expenses paid.

42. Smith dies. The mortgage company attempts to foreclose. Absent a statute governing their rights, what should happen?

A) The surviving joint tenant takes the tenancy subject to the mortgage.

B) The surviving joint tenant takes the tenancy free of the mortgage.

C) The mortgage company and Jones hold in joint tenancy.

D) Smith's heirs hold the undivided half subject to the debt.

43. In states that recognize common law dower, Smith marries Jones. He purchased Tanacre prior to his marriage, and during the marriage he purchased Bronzeacre. They separate. Smith sells both, and dies. What right does Jones have in each property?

A) Jones has dower in Tanacre, but not in Bronzeacre.

B) Jones has dower in Bronzeacre, but not in Tanacre.

C) Jones has dower in both.

D) Jones has dower in neither.

44. States that have abolished dower have generally replaced it with the following:

A) Community property system.

B) The elective share.

C) The homestead exemption.

D) Uniform Marital Property Act.

Questions 45–49 are based on these facts:

Smith and Jones married on January 1, 2009. Smith is a partner in a law firm. His salary for 2009 is $75,000 per year, and he received a $75,000 bonus on July 1, 2009. With his bonus, he bought 7,500 shares of X Corp in his own name, and received a dividend in December 2009 of $100. Jones's father died this year, and left her a bequest of $100,000. Her salary is $90,000 per year.

45. In a community property state, which of the following items are community property?

A) Smith's and Jones's salaries.

B) Smith's bonus.

C) X Corp dividend.

D) All of the above.

46. Smith dies in a community property state. In his will, he leaves all his property to the Red Cross. Of the following items, Smith's salary, his bonus, and his X Corp dividend, and Jones's inheritance and her salary, which items pass to the Red Cross?

A) Half of Smith's share of the community property.

B) All of the property allocated to Smith as his share of the community property acquired during marriage.

C) Smith's earnings, bonus, and dividends.

D) All, except that Jones gets her elective share in Smith's community property.

47. In a common law or separate property state, which items are separate property?

A) Smith's salary and bonus.

B) X Corp dividend.

C) Jones's salary and inheritance.

D) All of the above.

48. Smith dies in a common law property state. In his will, he leaves all his property (including an inheritance from his mother) to the Red Cross. Of the items mentioned above that are separate property and his inheritance, which pass to Red Cross?

A) All property passes to the Red Cross.

B) All property passes to the Red Cross subject to Jones's elective share.

C) All property passes to the Red Cross, except Smith's inheritance passes subject to Jones's elective share.

D) Half of all Smith's property passes to the Red Cross, the other half passes to Jones.

49. Suppose Smith and Jones were unmarried, but they lived together for 20 years. Which of the following arrangements would allow Smith to pass his estate to Jones at his death?

A) His will.

B) A contract to devise.

C) An *inter vivos* trust naming Smith life beneficiary, with the corpus to pass on his death to Jones.

D) All of the above.

50. What interest remains in the landlord who owns Tanacre in fee simple absolute when he makes a lease to Smith for 100 years?

A) A remainder.

B) A reversion.

C) A fee simple absolute.

D) An executory interest.

Questions 51–53 are based on these facts:

Smith owns a house, and agrees to lease it to Jones. The lease states that it will commence on July 4, 2004, but provides no termination date. Rent reserved is $1,000 per month.

51. What type of tenancy has been created?

A) A term of years.

B) A tenancy at will.

C) A month-to-month tenancy.

D) A tenancy at sufferance.

52. How can the tenant or the landlord terminate the lease?

A) Either party can terminate by giving the other party one month's notice.

B) Either party can terminate at the end of the one-year lease term.

C) The tenant may terminate the lease at any time.

D) The landlord may terminate the lease at any time.

53. Suppose the tenant's adult son lives in the house. The tenant dies on September 29. The tenant willed his entire estate to his son. What are the consequences of the tenant's death?

A) The lease terminates; the tenant's son must quit the premises.

B) The tenant's son may continue to live in the premises as long as he pays the rent, and neither the landlord nor the tenant's son give notice to quit.

C) The lease terminates only when the landlord learns of the tenant's death.

D) Nothing.

Questions 54–56 are based on these facts:

Suppose that the lease reads as follows: "this lease will commence on July 4, 2009 and terminate on January 4, 2010." The rent reserved is $1,000 per month.

54. What type of tenancy has been created?

A) A term of years.

B) A tenancy at will.

C) A periodic tenancy.

D) A tenancy at sufferance.

55. How can the tenant or the landlord terminate the lease?

A) Either party can terminate by giving the other party one month's notice.

B) Either party can terminate at the end of the lease term.

C) The tenant may terminate the lease at any time.

D) The lease terminates automatically at the end of the term.

56. On January 1, 2010, the landlord enters the leased premises with his key to show them to a prospective new tenant. Absent a provision to do so in the lease, is the landlord's action wrongful?

A) No, it is implied in the lease that landlord can show the premises to another prospective tenant.

B) No, landlords have a general right to inspect the premises.

C) Yes, the landlord has no right to enter the premises, absent the tenant's consent.

D) No, the landlord's act is not a substantial interference with the tenant's use since the tenant wasn't home.

Questions 57 and 58 are based on these facts:

Suppose the lease term is stated as follows: "this lease shall commence on July 4, 2009, and shall terminate immediately at any time by either party giving notice to the other party."

57. What type of tenancy has been created?

A) A term of years.

B) A tenancy at will.

C) A month-to-month tenancy.

D) A tenancy at sufferance.

58. Suppose the tenant's adult son lives in the house. The tenant dies on September 29. What are the consequences of his death?

A) The lease terminates; the tenant's son must quit the premises.

B) The tenant's son may continue to live in the premises as long as he pays the rent, and neither the landlord nor the tenant's son give notice to quit.

C) The lease terminates only when the landlord learns of the tenant's death.

D) Nothing.

59. Which of the following does the landlord not covenant in a lease?

A) Title.

B) Possession.

C) Quiet enjoyment.

D) Insurance.

60. If on the day that the lease commences, the previous tenant has not quit the premises, must the landlord take legal action to evict him and place the new tenant in actual physical possession?

A) Yes, in states that have adopted the Uniform Residential Landlord and Tenant Act.

B) Yes, under the common law of most American jurisdictions.

C) No, in states that have adopted the Uniform Residential Landlord and Tenant Act.

D) No, if the demised premises are for short-term furnished residential purposes.

Questions 61–63 are based on these facts:

Smith leases Tanacre to Jones. The ten-year lease has the following express provision: "the premises must be used for residential purposes as an apartment building." By year eight, the entire surrounding neighborhood has become commercial, and Jones is unable to find residential tenants. Jones asks Smith if he can convert the building into a hotel. Smith refuses, and threatens to terminate the lease if Jones rents to commercial tenants and to sue Jones for the rent for the remaining term.

61. What would be the tenant's best argument in defense?

A) Impossibility of performance.

B) Commercial frustration.

C) Breach of the implied warranty of suitability.

D) Breach of the implied warranty of habitability.

62. For the tenant to prevail in the above claim, which of the following would he have to prove?

A) That the landlord knew at the time the lease was executed that the neighborhood was going downhill.

B) That it was not reasonably foreseeable at the time the lease was executed that the use of the tenancy as apartments would be unprofitable.

C) That the landlord did not know that the neighborhood was declining.

D) That the landlord reasonably believed that using the tenancy as apartments would be profitable.

63. What would be the most appropriate remedy if the court found for the tenant?

A) Rescission of the lease.

B) Reformation of the "express purposes clause" to allow commercial tenants.

C) The difference between the rent reserved and the fair market value of the premises as a residential apartment.

D) The difference between the rent reserved and the fair market value of the premises as a commercial building.

Questions 64–66 are based on these facts:

Jones Enterprises owns residential apartments. In its advertisement in the "for rent" section of the newspaper, it advertises the Buckingham Arms as a quiet haven in the bustling city. Banks signs a one-year lease. Two weeks after moving in, Banks finds that the noise from his neighbor's television is unbearable.

64. Which of the following tenants' remedies should the tenant pursue?

A) Claim a constructive eviction, and rescission of the lease.

B) Raise the implied warranty of habitability.

C) Regard the lease as illegal.

D) Raise the implied warranty of suitability.

65. Which of the following would the tenant have to prove to prevail?

A) That the failure to keep the neighbors quiet was an obligation under the lease.

B) That the landlord had notice of the tenant's objections to the noise.

C) That the tenant moved out in a reasonable time after conditions deteriorated.

D) All of the above.

66. Which of the following would be an appropriate measure of damages should the tenant prevail?

A) Expenses in relocating.

B) The rental value of the new apartment over the term of the original lease with the landlord.

C) The value of the premises to the tenant.

D) The difference between the rent of a similar apartment without the unruly neighbors and the rent reserved over the term of the original lease with the landlord.

Questions 67–69 are based on these facts:

Suppose after living in the apartment for six months, the air conditioner no longer functions. Room temperature hovers around 90 degrees. The tenant informs the landlord, but the landlord fails to repair.

67. Which of the following causes of action should the tenant pursue?

A) Actual eviction.

B) Implied warranty of habitability.

C) Illegal lease.

D) Implied warranty of suitability.

68. Which of the following would the tenant have to prove to prevail?

A) That the failure to fix the air conditioning was an obligation under the lease.

B) That the lack of air conditioning rendered the premises unfit for human habitation.

C) That tenant moved out in a reasonable time.

D) All of the above.

69. Which of the following would NOT be an appropriate measure of damages should the tenant prevail?

A) Permitting the tenant to have the air conditioning fixed, and allowing the tenant to deduct the cost from the tenant's rent.

B) Requiring the tenant to pay a reduced rent.

C) The difference between the fair market value of the premises as warranted (with air conditioning) and the fair market value without air conditioning.

D) Allowing the tenant relocation expenses.

Questions 70 and 71 are based on these facts:

Jones enters into a ten-year commercial lease with Smith Enterprises. The landlord places the following clause in the lease: "Tenant agrees not to transfer the lease without the written consent of the Landlord." The agreed rent is $5,000 per month.

70. In year six, the tenant decides to retire. The tenant wishes to sublet or assign the premises to X Corp, a large multinational corporation that plans to use the premises for the same type of commercial enterprise as did the tenant. The landlord refuses to consent and to explain the reasons for his refusal. Is the landlord's action consistent with his obligations under the lease?

A) Yes, the landlord has reserved the right to consent to transfers.

B) Yes, unless the tenant can allege an oral agreement that limits the landlord's right to refuse.

C) No, regardless of the clause, the landlord cannot unreasonably refuse to allow a sublease assignment.

D) No, the lease does not expressly forbid transfers.

71. If the landlord is willing to allow the transfer, should the landlord insist on a sublet or an assignment?

A) A sublet, because then the landlord may sue both original tenant Jones and X Corp if the rent is not paid.

B) A sublet because the landlord may raise the rent.

C) An assignment, because then the landlord may sue both original tenant Jones and X Corp if the rent is not paid.

D) An assignment, because the landlord may raise the rent.

72. Which of the following statements best characterizes landlord tort liability?

A) Landlords are liable for damages for injuries sustained in common areas.

B) Landlords are liable for damages for injuries sustained from faulty repairs undertaken.

C) Landlords are liable for damages for injuries sustained from concealed defects of which the landlord was aware.

D) All of the above.

73. Under the common law of nuisance in American courts, which of the following principles were not generally recognized?

A) First in time, first in right.

B) Common-enemy rule.

C) Ancient lights.

D) The right of downstream riparian owners to receive a flow of water.

74. Under the Restatement (Second) of Torts §§821 et seq., which of the following elements need not be proven by the plaintiff suing in nuisance?

A) That the plaintiff has an interest in land that has been invaded by the defendant.

B) That the defendant's act or omission caused an intentional invasion of the plaintiff's interest in land.

C) That the plaintiff was using her property prior to the point in time in which the defendant began to cause the invasion.

D) That the defendant's conduct was unreasonable.

75. Again, under the Restatement, what factor renders an actor's conduct unreasonable?

A) When the gravity of the harm caused by the actor to another exceeds its social utility.

B) When she acts recognizing that her conduct is injurious to others.

C) When she acts for the purpose of causing harm.

D) When a jury in considering the circumstances finds the actor's conduct wrongful.

Questions 76–78 are based on these facts:

In 1990, Smith Enterprises erected a brick-making factory three miles from the Town of Bliss. Over the ensuing decade, suburbs of Bliss have now reached the factory's border. Jones purchased property adjacent to the factory, and built her family home on the site. The factory, which had only one shift, has now added an evening shift. Jones brings an action to enjoin the use of the factory entirely or to get damages, because it is noisy and pollutes.

76. Should plaintiff Jones prevail?

A) Yes, there is an invasion of plaintiff's property.

B) No, the factory was there first.

C) No, the gravity of the harm to plaintiff outweighs the social utility of the factory's conduct.

D) Yes, the harm is serious, but the factory could continue to operate and compensate plaintiff for damages.

77. Should plaintiff's claim prevail, which would be the most efficient remedy?

   A) An injunction against further operation of the factory.

   B) Permanent damages.

   C) Relocation expenses.

   D) All of the above.

78. Suppose the factory agrees to install filters to diminish the output of dust to near zero, but cannot curtail the noise very much given the state of noise abatement technology. In considering whether its conduct is actionable, which of the following should be considered?

   A) Whether the factory operates according to a fixed schedule.

   B) Whether the factory is operating in good faith.

   C) Whether the factory has made every effort to abate the unreasonable invasion.

   D) Whether noise is an invasion.

79. Which of the following is not an easement?

   A) The right held by the owner of Tanacre to cross Bronzeacre to reach her garage.

   B) The right held by the owner of Tanacre to prevent the owner of Bronzeacre to use her land for commercial purposes.

   C) The right of the owner of Tanacre to use a drive partly on her own land and partly on the land of Bronzeacre.

   D) The right of a person to fish in Bronzeacre Lake.

Questions 80–84 are based on these facts:

   Smith and Jones are adjoining landowners. A dirt road has long been located on Smith's land, about four feet from the boundary between the two plots. Five years ago, Jones decided to construct a house on her previously vacant lot. Jones asked Smith if her construction team could use the road for building equipment access. Smith agreed. The road was used during the building of her house. Jones continued to use the road for day-to-day access, and last year Jones asked Smith if Jones could pave it at Jones's own expense. Shortly thereafter Jones had the road paved. Last month, Banks bought Smith's land and blocked Jones's access.

80. If an easement was indeed created, how was it created?

   A) By grant.

   B) By prescription.

C) By necessity.

D) By estoppel.

81. If an easement was created, can Banks enjoin Jones's use?

A) No, the burden of the easement runs with Smith's parcel.

B) No, the benefit of the easement runs with Jones's parcel.

C) Yes, the burden is personal; it can only be enforced against Smith.

D) Yes, the benefit terminated when Smith sold his land to Banks.

82. If an easement was created, can Jones's guests also use the drive to reach her house?

A) Yes, if such use was in the contemplation of Smith and Jones when they agreed to her use of the drive.

B) Yes, if Jones's guests had used the drive while Smith owned the servient parcel.

C) No, only the holder of an easement can use an easement.

D) No, easements are personal.

83. Suppose Banks now also decides to buy the Jones parcel. He then grants the same parcel to Norris without mentioning the easement. Is the original Smith parcel subject to the easement?

A) No, the easement was terminated by merger when Banks held both the original Smith and Jones parcels.

B) No, unless Banks was using the drive to reach the land previously owned by Jones.

C) Yes, the easement will be implied in the grant to Norris.

D) Yes, easements run with the land.

84. Suppose that before selling, Jones decides to use her parcel for commercial purposes. She builds a group of five small hunting lodges on her parcel. The hunters use the drive. Which of the following arguments might Banks (owning the original Smith parcel) successfully use to stop them?

A) The easement was terminated by misuse.

B) Excessive overuse terminates an easement.

C) Use beyond the scope of the easement can be enjoined.

D) The easement was terminated by merger.

85. Which of the requirements for the creation of an easement by implication are not required for the creation of an easement by necessity?

A) Unity of title.

B) Severance.

C) Necessity.

D) Apparent use so as to constitute notice.

86. Smith and Jones are neighbors. Smith is to the west; Jones to the east. For over 20 years, Smith has had a pool in his yard, which has received morning sunlight over the Jones parcel unimpeded, when the sun and clouds cooperate. After a falling out, Jones proceeds to build a fence on his side of the property line that "shadows" Smith's pool for about four hours in the morning. What would be the best legal argument for Smith to use to seek damages or require Jones to tear down his fence?

A) Smith claims a negative easement by prescription.

B) Smith claims ancient lights.

C) Smith claims Jones has erected a spite fence.

D) That the gravity of the harm of the fence to Smith's property outweighs its social utility.

Questions 87–92 are based on these facts:

Joes's Bar has operated in the same premises for the past 40 years. Business is good, and Joe wants to move three blocks north to a larger venue. He conveys the building he owns to Banks and places the following restriction in the deed: "vendee agrees not to use the premises as a bar."

87. Banks uses the premises as a flower shop. Business is not good and a year later he opens a bar. Joe sues to enjoin the use of the premises as a bar. How would Joe's lawyer likely characterize the use restriction?

A) A covenant.

B) A possibility of reverter.

C) A right of entry for condition broken.

D) An easement.

88. If Joe sued Banks to enjoin Banks from using the premises as a bar, which of the following would be Banks's best argument in defense?

A) He was not in horizontal privity with Joe.

B) He was not in vertical privity with Joe.

C) The covenant does not touch and concern the land.

D) None of the above.

89. Suppose instead of using the premises as a bar, Banks sold the premises to Norris, who uses the premises as a bar. May Joe enjoin Norris's use?

A) Yes, if the requirements of an equitable servitude are met.

B) Yes, if the restriction was intended to bind successors.

C) No, there is no privity between Norris and Banks.

D) No, there is no privity between Joe and Norris.

90. Could Joe sue Norris at law for damages in the amount of his lost profits occasioned since Norris opened his bar?

A) No, equitable servitudes are enforced only through injunctions.

B) No, there is no privity between Norris and Banks.

C) Yes, if the elements of a real covenant can be met.

D) Yes, covenants not to compete can be enforced as equitable servitudes in an action for damages.

91. Suppose Joe decides to seek damages. Which of the following may Norris raise in defense?

A) That the covenant does not specifically state that it binds successors, a requirement for the enforceability of a promise against successors as a real covenant.

B) That covenants not to compete are always personal.

C) That covenants not to compete can only be enforced against the promisor.

D) That Norris and Joe are not in horizontal privity.

92. Suppose Joe sells his new bar to Manny, who sells to Moe. Can Moe enforce the promise against Norris as either a real covenant or an equitable servitude?

A) No, only the original promisee can enforce promises that run with land.

B) Yes, successors in interest to promisee can enforce promises against successors in interest to promisor if the requirements of a real covenant or equitable servitude are met.

C) Yes, so long as the touch and concern requirement is met.

D) No, the promise can be enforced only against the original promisor.

93. Which of the following planned uses for land pass the "public use" test set out by the Supreme Court in establishing guidelines for the exercise of eminent domain?

A) A post office.

B) A state courthouse.

C) A multiuse urban renewal project.

D) All of the above.

94. In the *Kelo v. City of New London* case, the *dissent* stressed what aspect of the project and its consequences to find that the city of New London exceeded its powers of eminent domain?

A) That some of the property taken was not blighted.

B) That the city was acting in bad faith.

C) That "due process" was not accorded the property holders.

D) That the project provided no reciprocity of advantage to the property holders.

95. For which of the following would Joe of Joe's Bar above NOT be compensated if his land was taken by eminent domain to build a highway?

A) The fair market value of the land taken.

B) The fixtures on the land.

C) Relocation expenses and lost profits during the relocation period.

D) The fair market value of the building on the premises.

96. Suppose Joe owned the bar in fee simple, but leased it to Manny. Ten years remained on the lease. Who would receive just compensation and for what interests?

A) Joe takes the entire amount.

B) Manny takes the entire amount.

C) Joe and Manny divide the amount; Manny receives the value of the lease, and Joe the remaining value.

D) Joe and Manny divide the amount; Joe gets the value of property and Manny gets the value of the fixtures.

97. Under what circumstances does a government regulation always require that the landowner be paid just compensation?

A) Where there is an average reciprocity of advantage.

B) Where the government conditions the approval of a use of the premises, but requires the landowner to grant some benefit to the public.

C) Where the regulation requires a permanent physical occupation of the land.

D) Where the value of the land has been reduced by the regulation.

Questions 98–101 are based on these facts:

Smith bought a large beachfront tract of land on a barrier island off the coast of Atlantis in 2005. He bought the property to develop the land. A year or so later as lot prices climbed, he thought about subdividing the land into two beachfront lots, a proposal that did not require planning permission. He dithers. In 2008, Atlantis passed a law that prohibited, among other things, the subdivision of any lots on the beach. The prohibition lasts three years.

98. Smith brings action in federal court claiming that a regulatory taking has occurred. Which argument best supports his takings claim?

A) His primary expectations for the land have been thwarted.

B) The use of his land, two houses, was not regarded as a nuisance at common law.

C) A three-year prohibition is tantamount to a permanent taking of his right to develop.

D) Not being able to subdivide is tantamount to the government occupying one-half of his land.

99. Suppose instead of preventing the subdivision, Smith was permitted to subdivide, but was required to deed a strip of land to the public for access to the beach. Which argument best supports a takings claim?

A) The requirement would be an unconstitutional condition and therefore requires just compensation, because subdividing his land does not make it more difficult for the public to access the beach.

B) The requirement requires just compensation because it thwarts his investment-backed expectations.

C) The requirement requires just compensation because the public is in possession permanently of part of his land.

D) The requirement requires just compensation because the strip of land has been rendered valueless to him.

100. If Smith was able to place a gate on the strip, and allow access only on an occasional basis when the public beaches were not crowded, what argument might the government make to support its claim that there was not a taking?

A) That there was no taking of the strip because Smith could control time, place, and manner of public access.

B) That there was no taking of the strip because the gate gave him an average reciprocity of advantage.

C) That there was no taking of the strip because Smith's investment-backed expectations were now preserved.

D) That there was no taking of the strip because Smith's land lost no value.

101. Which set of cases best illustrates how the composition of the Supreme Court has impacted the outcome of regulatory takings cases?

A) *Loretto* and *Penn Central*.

B) *Penn Coal* and *Keystone Coal*.

C) *Penn Central* and *Penn Coal*.

D) *Penn Central* and *Lucas*.

102. *Euclid v. The Village of Ambler* is the central case in zoning law for which of the following reasons?

A) It upheld the constitutionality of Ambler's zoning master plan as applied to property owned by Euclid.

B) It determined that the principle of zoning was a valid exercise of the police power and therefore some limitation on land use by an owner of land might not be a taking.

C) It determined that zoning plans may devalue some private property rights.

D) It questioned whether particular parcels of Euclid's land had been taken without just compensation.

103. Smith has run a convenience store on unzoned land. The town zoning board reclassified his property, and that of neighboring businesses, as "low-income residential" last month. Which factors should a zoning board NOT take into account in determining whether and for how long each business affected may operate as a non-conforming use?

A) The value of each property.

B) The social utility of the business affected.

C) Height and density of the structures.

D) The proximity of the store to other stores.

104. What response best describes the United States Supreme Court's most recent pronouncements on the state's or municipalities' ability to zone out adult bookstores/entertainment venues?

A) A community may zone adult bookstores/entertainment venues into high-crime areas.

B) A community may zone out entirely adult bookstores/entertainment venues.

C) A community may limit adult bookstores/entertainment venues if it believes that they contribute to crime.

D) A community may limit adult bookstores/entertainment venues if a survey shows that there is a link between high crime and adult bookstores/entertainment.

105. Which of the following zoning ordinances should be held invalid under current Supreme Court jurisprudence?

A) Those that prohibit unrelated individuals from living together in areas zoned single family residential only.

B) Those that exclude multigenerational families from living together in areas zoned single family residential only.

C) Those that exclude sorority sisters from living together in areas zoned single family residential only.

D) Those that prohibit members of a religious community from living together with families in areas zoned single family residential only.

106. Which of the following is true of zoning plans that exclude provision for low-income housing?

A) They violate the Equal Protection Clause of the United States Constitution.

B) They violate the Fair Housing Act.

C) They violate the constitution of most American states.

D) They violate the constitution of a few American states.

107. Which of the following NEED NOT be proved in order to receive a variance from a zoning regulation?

A) The granting of the variance would not be incompatible with the comprehensive plan.

B) The landowner will suffer a unique hardship owing to the zoning.

C) The landowner holds the only lot that will be detrimentally affected.

D) The hardship is unnecessary because it will not be suffered if the variance is granted.

Questions 108–111 are based on these facts:

On July 4, 2008, Smith orally agreed to purchase Tanacre from Jones for $5,000 on July 30. Jones agreed to produce a contract for sale by the 14th. The following day

Smith posted a check to Jones in the amount of $2,500. Smith then approached Bank Zero for a loan commitment for $4,000, secured on the premises. On the 14th, Jones tore up Smith's check and signed a contract with Norris to sell Tanacre for $6,000.

108. May Smith sue Jones for damages?

A) No, the transaction does not satisfy the Statute of Frauds.

B) No, a seller can always refuse to close until a contract is signed.

C) Yes, receipt of the deposit precludes a sale to a third party.

D) Yes, Smith having partially performed his obligations, equity will order specific performance.

109. Suppose when Smith sent the check to Jones he wrote on the reverse of the check the following: "deposit for one-half the purchase price of Tanacre, remaining sum to be paid by closing July 30 subject to financing." Prior to Jones cashing the check, does the check itself satisfy the Statute of Frauds?

A) Yes, it contains all the essential information required by the statute.

B) Yes, the receipt of the check with a summary of the agreed terms satisfies the statute.

C) No, Jones not having cashed the check, there is no unequivocal indication that the seller has agreed to the terms set out on the reverse of the check.

D) No, a deposit check can never constitute a sales contract under the statute because it is signed only by the buyer.

110. Which of the following would had to have occurred to make the oral agreement enforceable?

A) Jones cashed the check.

B) Smith paid Jones the entire sale price in cash before the contract with Norris was signed.

C) Smith signed a contract with a builder, Banks, to build a house on Tanacre.

D) Smith's builder entered into the premises unbeknownst to Jones and began to construct the house.

111. Suppose instead of the above arm's length transaction, Smith had agreed to care for Jones for the rest of Jones's life, in return for an option to buy the property for $2,000 less than appraised fair market value at Jones's death. Would this oral agreement be enforceable at Jones's death assuming performance by Smith?

A) Yes, the statute does not apply in respect of partially gratuitous transfers.

B) Yes, equitable estoppel applies.

C) No, the terms of the oral agreement are not specific as to price.

D) No, the agreement violates public policy.

112. After the sales contract for purchase of residential property, which of the following circumstances, if undisclosed by the seller, would make the title no longer "marketable"?

A) All deeds in the chain of title have residential restrictions.

B) All deeds in the chain of title have single family dwelling — only restrictions.

C) The property is zoned single family residential.

D) The house on the property does not meet building code standards.

113. Which of the following defects in deeds would render title not marketable?

A) A previous deed in the chain of title misdescribes the property subject to the contract.

B) The guardian of the minor titleholder has executed a previous deed in the chain of title, and the minor has not joined.

C) A previous deed in the chain of title includes a testamentary transmission.

D) A previous deed in the chain of title has a corporate owner, and only an officer has executed the deed.

Questions 114 and 115 are based on these facts:

On July 4, 2009, Smith as vendor and Jones as vendee enter into a contact for the sale of Tanacre. Jones pays a down payment of one-third the purchase price of $100,000.

114. Two weeks later, a mudslide destroys the house and renders the lot uninhabitable. If Jones refuses to close, may Smith seek specific performance?

A) Yes, in most states under the doctrine of equitable conversion.

B) Yes, but only if he was unaware that the property was susceptible to mudslides.

C) No, unless Smith misrepresented the topography.

D) No, in most states under the doctrine of equitable conversion.

115. Suppose the mudslide occurs and renders both the house and lot uninhabitable. Which of the following would preclude a claim by Smith for specific performance?

A) There was a clause allowing the buyer to void the contract if the premises were damaged by an act of God.

B) Smith continued to hold a casualty insurance policy on the premises.

C) Jones had taken out a casualty insurance policy on the premises.

D) Jones had taken out a casualty insurance policy on the premises to commence on the closing date.

PROPERTY
MULTIPLE CHOICE
ANSWERS & ANALYSIS

PROPERTY ANSWERS AND ANALYSIS

1. Issue: Characterization of property

The correct answer is **B**. The property should be characterized as mislaid. Because people generally do not part with valuable property, courts rarely find property to be "abandoned" D (owner voluntarily relinquishes her right). The property, though old, is not that old, and was not found in the ground; hence it is unlikely to be considered "treasure trove" C. Because it must have been placed in the book, it was not "lost," where possessor or owner accidentally parts with possession. The property was mislaid, because the circumstances in which it was found suggest that the bond was placed in the book, and its whereabouts forgotten by the owner.

2. Issue: Characterization of rights by holder

The correct answer is **B**. Jones is a possessor. Ownership of the book, rather like ownership of land, conveys constructive possession of that which is within the pages. But not when there is clearly another owner. The owner of the bond is Sergeant Westcott, or if he is dead, his heirs or legatees A. Jones is not a finder, because he never seems to have been aware that the bond was in the book C. He is not a bailee D because a prior possessor did not voluntarily deliver property to him.

3. Issue: Priority of rights

The correct answer is **C**. The court should award the bond to Wescott or his heirs. The finder of property, here Smith, has rights against all but the true owner. Having paid value for the bond, Westcott is or was the owner (a). If he is dead, it ought to go to his heirs (or devisees under his will). The U.S. government (d) has no right in the bond; it is merely Westcott's debtor. While Jones has a right in the property as a prior possessor (b), his right is inferior to that of the true owner.

4. Issue: Rights of bona fide purchasers

The correct answer is **B**. Wescott or his heirs may recover against Smith, but not Banks. Banks A and C is a bona fide purchaser for value, and therefore has good title under Uniform Commercial Code §2-403(1). Smith did not come into possession of the property wrongfully; he therefore had at least voidable title, allowing him to pass good title to one who believes he is purchasing from an individual with good title. But since Wescott's heirs have a greater right in the property than did Smith, and they attempt to assert it, they ought to be able to recover its value from Smith.

5. Issue: Creation of bailments

The correct answer is **B**. A bailment has been created. A bailment is a voluntary transfer and delivery by a possessor of property (bailor) to another (bailee) for safekeeping, and with the expectation that the property will be returned upon request. Smith expected both printing and return of the film negatives. It was not a gift C because, though there was delivery, there was no donative intent; neither party believed that the camera shop would keep the negatives. A trust A was not created; trusts are created when a party expressly undertakes a fiduciary obligation to hold legal title for the benefit of a third party. There was no intent expressed to create a trust; no words establishing a trust were used. Conversion can occur when a party exercises ownership rights over the property of another without consent D. Here Smith voluntarily handed over the film to the clerk.

6. Issue: Bailor's remedy for loss of bailed property

The correct answer is **A**. Smith will be able to claim A. In bailments, the bailor expects the return of the property bailed. Generally, bailees are strictly liable for failure to redeliver bailed property. So the bailor must only redeliver the undeveloped film? Not in this case. An exception is made where the bailor expects the property to be processed. Here Smith handed over exposed film; he expected the return of a processed product: negative and prints. But since he has not paid for the prints he cannot receive B. Absent agreement, bailees are not responsible for consequential damages; thus he cannot receive either the value of his trip C or a return trip D.

7. Issue: Bailee's disclaimer

The correct answer is **A**. The camera store may still be liable for A. The camera store attempted to limit its liability in the event it lost or damaged the film. It will argue that the bailment was subject to the express condition. While a court may enforce the exculpatory clause, it may not absolve the camera store from negligent conduct. Thus the standard may be altered from strict liability to negligence. Losing the film while in the store probably meets that standard. The same logic in Question 6 above applies to B, C, and D.

8. Issue: The application of law of capture

The correct answer is **D**. The court in the Barry Bonds baseball case (*Popov v. Hayashi*), *Hammonds v. Central Kentucky Natural Gas* C, and *E. A. Stephens and Co. v. Albers* D applied the law of capture.

9. Issue: Common law right of publicity

The correct answer is **D**. While movie stars B, political figures C, and indeed mere mortals A may claim the right, the individual so claiming must exploit his or her persona for material gain.

10. Issue: Intellectual property

The correct answer is **C**. Merely reporting a viewed news item, even if copyrighted, does not violate rights A, though between competitors, following *INS v. AP*, CNN might raise unfair competition claim B. But the parties here are not engaged in a similar enterprise. Broadcasting is not a waiver D; at the end of the programs there is generally notice of a claim of copyright.

11. Issue: Copyright

The correct answer is **D**. Photocopying the odd page of copyrighted material for academic use is within the "fair use" exception A. Not the whole volume, please. The fact that the author retells a well-worn tale, like the structure of the court system C is not dispositive, if her rendition is creative. Theft is not relevant B though the reproduction of some copyrighted materials (particularly movies) are covered by IP-related misappropriation crimes.

12. Issue: Adverse possession theory

The correct answer is **C**. Fearful that someone may believe that undeveloped land is free for the taking, an owner might want to discourage adverse use by developing, leading to another unnecessary strip mall. A and B are incorrect because they are efficiency explanations. It is doubtful that allowing adverse possession promotes suits D, though it does prompt a vigilant landowner to bring an action to eject a "squatter."

13. Issue: Continuous use

The correct answer is **C**. For a possessor to perfect a claim of adverse possession, the adverse possessor's occupation must be actual, open and notorious, continuous, exclusive, and adverse. Because Bloggs has made an entry onto the land (he lives there), he is in actual possession A. His possession is open and notorious B because he has made no attempt to conceal it, so that a reasonably vigilant owner would know of his entry. It is exclusive D because he does not appear to be using the property in concert with others or with the titleholder. However, it may not be continuous because he uses the property seasonally, rather than for the entire year C.

14. Issue: Adverse possession

The correct answer is **C**. Even a brief period of use by the land titleholder is generally held sufficient to break both the continuous and exclusive requirements for adverse possession; B and D are therefore incorrect. Arguably the titleholder is monitoring his land, by posting "no trespassing" signs. By exercising his ownership rights, Jones has made clear he intends to protect his right in the land. For Bloggs's use to no longer be adverse A, Jones had to have given Bloggs permission.

15. Issue: Tacking

The correct answer is **D**. Successive possessors may tack years of possession to reach the statute of limitations if the successive possessors were in privity of estate. So Bloggs, Jr. does not have to be in possession for 20 years A. In order to meet that requirement, possession has to be transferred from one possessor to the next through a legally recognized transfer such as a contract for sale, gift, or a will. Thus the 15 years Bloggs held can be used by Bloggs, Jr. to meet the 20-year limitation. While it is true that Bloggs, Jr. may have "inherited" C the years Bloggs had accumulated, it is the concept of tacking that allows Bloggs, Jr. to add them to her own years of possession to meet the statutory period. It is not correct to say that she must be in possession for the full 20 years A. An adverse possessor is never in privity with the titleholder B.

16. Issue: Change of land ownership

The correct answer is **B**. Tacking (and therefore privity) is only necessary when adverse possessors come and go, not when the property occupied is transferred A and C. Adverse possession observes the conduct of the adverse possessor: has her conduct met the standard of actual possession, open, notorious, continuous, exclusive, and adverse. If the titleholder does not protect his right, adverse possession is perfected. So long as the subsequent owner of the property had a reasonable time period to object to the adverse possessor's use of the land, the adverse possessor may bring an action to quiet title against the second owner. An adverse possessor is never in privity with the titleholder D.

17. Issue: Adversity requirement

The correct answer is **D**. Many courts delve into the state of mind of the adverse possessor. Under the Maine rule, the adverse possessor must be subjectively hostile; she must know the property is not hers. Here Bloggs actually believes that he is occupying the land of his brother, presumably with his permission, and therefore is not hostile or adverse; under the Maine formulation he would lose A. Other jurisdictions require subjective good faith: that the occupier has reason to believe that he has a legal right in the property. Merely thinking the property is his brother's is insufficient unless he has some objective basis. Thus Bloggs is not acting in "good faith" under the Iowa formulation, and would therefore lose B. A third group of jurisdictions do not delve into the occupier's intent; they find the adversity requirement fulfilled by the objective fact of occupation C. Under this last formulation, Bloggs would prevail.

18. Issue: Waste

The correct answer is **D**. A life tenant has a limited interest in the tenancy, and must deliver the premises to the reversioner or holder of the succeeding interest in the same condition as she received it. Another way of characterizing the obligation is that the life tenant may not undertake acts that devalue the property. In each example, the value of the premises is diminished. The oil A or residence B is no longer an element of value in the land, and these answers are therefore incorrect. Arguably the shopping center is an improvement; but because at the time that the residence is torn down, the positive economic effect is speculative, the act still probably constitutes waste C.

19. Issue: Defeasible fees

The correct answer is **B**. There are two types of traditional conditional fee simple estates in land: the fee simple determinable and the fee simple on a condition subsequent. They differ from the fee simple absolute (to *A* and her heirs) in that the grantor has subjected the estate to a use limitation A. While the magic words actually used frequently direct the categorization of the conditional fee (fee simple determinable "so long as," fee simple on a condition subsequent "but if"), the real issue is whether the grantor provided for an automatic cessation of the interest in the grantee, and return of the estate to the grantor or her heirs; or an optional one, that the grantor may re-enter the premises, and take the possessory interest from the grantee if he so desires. Here the words suggest automatic rather than optional cessation D, and therefore a fee simple determinable in Jones with a possibility of reverter in Smith, and not a right of entry C.

20. Issue: Defeasible fees

The correct answer is **A**. In the traditional defeasible fee simples B, C, and D, the future interest is retained by the grantor. Here it is transferred in the grant; it does not take effect at the natural termination of the preceding estate, so it is an executory interest.

21. Issue: Fee simple absolute

The correct answer is **C**. In order to create a fee simple absolute, the grantor was required to use the proper words of limitation: to Jones and his heirs A. Failure to do so would vest a present possessory life estate in the grantee. Creation of a fee simple determinable occurred when the grantor subjected the property to a use limitation B. A fee tail required the use of the limitation to Jones and the heirs of her body D.

22. Issue: Fee simple absolute

The correct answer is **A**. Most modern courts would look to form rather than substance: what did the grantor intend? Most likely the greatest interest, the fee simple absolute.

23. Issue: Future interests

The correct answer is **C**. The interest takes effect at the natural termination of a simultaneously created estate and is therefore a remainder, but it is subject to a condition precedent: Jones surviving Smith. Thus it is not vested A. Executory interests B divest other interests, which is not the case here. Possibility of reverters D are retained when fee simple determinable is created.

24. Issue: Future interests

The correct answer is **B**. The estate remains in the grantor until the event occurs, "springing" into possession out of the estate of the grantor or his heirs. Had the grantor limited the estate to another ("to *A* and her heirs, then . . .") it would have been a shifting executory interest D. The interest cannot be a remainder A or C because it "cuts short" an interest.

25. Issue: Future interests

The correct answer is **A**. Amy has a vested life estate in remainder (the limitation is to a certain person, Amy, to become possessory on an event certain to occur, the death of Smith); no event need occur for her to enjoy the estate so it is not contingent. Her children as yet unborn have a contingent remainder; the limitation is uncertain persons, to children unborn, and perhaps never born. Thus any response B through D is incorrect. Jones's interest is an executory interest and not a contingent remainder (taking effect in possession upon passing the bar), because it will cut short an interest, and not become possessory at the natural termination of a simultaneously created estate.

26. Issue: Future interests

The correct answer is **B**. Amy's vested remainder becomes a present possessory estate at the termination of its supporting estate. But the quality of her estate is an estate for her life as specified in the limitation. The remainder was already vested, because the limitation is to a certain person, Amy, to become possessory on an event certain to occur, the death of Smith A. A fee simple absolute endures forever, and not for the life of an individual C.

27. Issue: Future interests

The correct answer is **D**. The birth of Bertha causes the contingent remainder to vest both subject to open (in the event that Amy has further children) and divestment (Jones passes the bar). But once born, the interest in the child vests, and should that child die, the interest passes to her heirs: there are no words of divestment. The birth of Bertha has no effect on the interests of Amy or Jones. These interests endure or fail according to their own terms A and B.

28. Issue: Future interests

The correct answer is **C**. Under the terms of the limitation, the interest in Jones, the executory interest, immediately becomes possessory upon passage of the bar. Thus the vested remainder subject to divestment and open is divested A, and the possessory estate in Amy is terminated immediately; she does not continue to enjoy it until her death D. Right to possession passes to Jones B.

29. Issue: Future interests

The correct answer is **A**. Upon the death of Amy, the vested remainder subject to divestment and open closes, and becomes a possessory fee simple absolute in the described taker, Bertha. Jones has not met the condition for the executory interest that would have shifted the estate to him, passing the bar in the lifetime of Amy.

30. Issue: Future interests

The correct answer is **B**. The limitation requires that condition of the executory interest (Jones passing the bar) be met before Amy's death. On Amy's death Bertha (and any other children of Amy, or if deceased their issue), share the estate in fee simple absolute, and not only for her life C.

31. Issue: Future interests

The correct answer is **C**. The grant is clear (so A is incorrect); there is no need to imply anything. B is incorrect because the interest in Jones was not a

contingent remainder. The interest in Jones must vest or fail during his life, a
life in being at the time of the grant, so there is no perpetuities problem D.

32. Issue: Merger

The correct answer is **B**. Merger occurs when the same person holds a vested
estate and the *next succeeding* vested estate (not the next A). When Carly buys
Amy's life interest she holds a vested life estate, and a vested remainder, with a
contingent estate in Bertha between the two. Merger of the two vested estates
squeezes out Bertha's contingent interest. Neither the Rule in Shelly's Case
nor the Doctrine of Worthier Title apply. The first applies when a conveyance
grants a life estate to Amy and a remainder to her heirs C. The grant in the
question creates a fee simple in Amy. The latter holds that when a grantor (G)
makes a grant of a life interest to another with a remainder to the grantor's heirs
(to *A* for life, then to *G*'s heirs), the grantor's heirs take nothing and the grantor
retains a reversion D.

33. Issue: Rule against perpetuities

The correct answer is **B**. The rule against perpetuities applies only to
contingent interests. Reversions D, rights of entry C, and vested remainders
A are considered vested interests.

34. Issue: Rule against perpetuities

The correct answer is **D**. Amy has a vested life estate; Bertha a springing
executory interest in fee simple. The latter must vest or fail within the
period of the rule, a life in being plus 21 years. Though unlikely, Amy
could die, grief-stricken Bertha could die the following day, and the sloth-
ful executor might take more than 21 years to probate the estate. Thus the
act that causes the interest to vest *might* vest longer than a life in being plus
21 years. That Bertha is dead is irrelevant: the interest is in fee simple, and
would vest in the heirs of Bertha if she was dead at the time the contin-
gency occurs.

35. Issue: Rule against perpetuities

The correct answer is **D**. Other than Amy's interest, the interests are
contingent, and therefore may be subject to the rule against perpetuities.
They take effect with uncertain persons, a widower, and children living at
the time of the death of Amy and the widower. Although Boris is alive, he may
die, and Amy may marry a man, Edgar, who is not born at the time of the grant.
While the gift to him must vest or fail on the death of Amy, a life in being, the
gift to the children vests at his death, which may occur more than 21 years after
a life in being at the time of the grant. So here's what might happen: Clare and
David may die, and after the grant Amy may have a son Frank; Boris dies and
Amy marries Edgar, a chap who was born (improbably though possibly) after
the grant; Edgar survives Amy, Clare, and David by more than 21 years, and
then dies. The gift then vests in Frank more than 21 years after some life in
being at the time of the grant.

s

ring the remainder limited to a person now
n be measuring lives. The remainder in the
ail in the couple's lifetimes. The limitation to
of Amy" doesn't help. First, she must marry
d second, the perpetuities period runs from
ne that he must be in being to be a measuring
dower A is vested subject to divestment and

s

ders may be limited to children yet unborn,
e in being and 21 years. In order for the
n the perpetuities period, they must vest or
hoice B is incorrect because the interest vests
g widow, who might be unborn at the time
ldren at the time of the grant may die, the
g year Amy has another child. The gift then
an 21 years after a life in being.

;

iandful of states retain the rule in its pristine
:s invalidates all future interests in a grant if
ilates the rule. Under the "wait and see"
: if they actually vest during the perpetuities
he interest in Amy's children would not fail
vas born after the grant. Under cy pres, the
n as granting the remainder to only spouses
States that implement USRAP set a time
nterests to vest or fail, a likely occurrence

ould probably conclude that a joint tenancy
ire a particular form of concurrent owner-
undivided half interest; at the death of the
rvivor owns the entire interest. Usually
urvivorship" appear in the limitation, but
:o suggest that the survivor should own the
ie first to die. A tenancy by the entirety is a
ween spouses B. A tenancy in common is a
iich the surviving joint tenant does not take
e C. Thus the use of the word "survivor"
common. D is incorrect both because
estate known to the law, and Smith has

40. Issue: Joint estates

The correct answer is **B**. Unmarried individuals can hold property in joint tenancy; the divorce has no effect on the title C. Even without consent, a mortgage undertaken by a joint tenant does not sever the joint tenancy A or D, because in most states, the title to the mortgage property remains with the mortgagor, and the debt is a lien on the property. Severance would only occur on foreclosure. In some states, however, the mortgagee does take title subject to the mortgagor's equity of redemption. In these states (few in number), title is no longer (at least in theory) in the joint tenants, but courts in these jurisdictions recognize the ownership in the mortgagee as a legal fiction.

41. Issue: Joint estates

The correct answer is **A**. Joint tenants are responsible for their share of the tax liability of the joint tenancy. Taxes are an obligation on the owners. However, the joint tenant is not obligated to repair or to pay other expenses B, C, or D; if Smith does so Smith cannot charge the other joint tenant.

42. Issue: Joint estates

The correct answer is **B**. Because the undivided half interest of the mortgagor no longer exists, the mortgage company has no recourse in a lien theory state. The debt does not pass to the survivor when the interest of the deceased joint tenant passes A, because legally speaking the deceased joint tenant's interest doesn't pass C. The deceased's undivided half ceases to exist, as does the secured debt D. For this reason it is prudent for a lender to have both joint tenants take out the mortgage.

43. Issue: Dower rights

The correct answer is **C**. At common law, dower attaches to all real property that the husband was seised of at anytime during the marriage. Unless the wife released her dower, she has a right to the dower in both parcels.

44. Issue: Dower rights

The correct answer is **B**. In most jurisdictions, the elective share has replaced dower. Both real and personal property are subject to the elective share. Eight states have the community property A system, derived from continental jurisdictions in which dower was not present. Only Wisconsin has adopted the UMPA D. The homestead exemption is a right granted to the surviving spouse to live in the marital home or receive a specified payment from the estate C.

45. Issue: Community property

The correct answer is **D**. In community property states, earnings including bonuses are community property. Dividends on community property are community property. One-half of the earnings, bonus, and dividends are allocated to him; one-half to Jones.

46. Issue: Community property

The correct answer is **B**. Because community property regimes allocate one-half of the spouse's earnings during marriage, spouses can devise their entire share of the community property as they wish. Thus *all* his share of the community property (not one-half A; not all his earnings, bonus, and dividends C) can be willed to the Red Cross. Jones's inheritance is her own separate property, and Smith has no elective share right in a community property jurisdiction D.

47. Issue: Common law separate property

The correct answer is **D**. Earnings, bonuses A (and proceeds thereof B), and inheritances received C are separate property. The other spouse has no interest in any of the items listed.

48. Issue: Common law separate property

The correct answer is **B**. In separate property states (with the exception of Georgia), the surviving spouse has the right to elect against the will, and receive a proportion of the deceased spouse's probate estate. All of the property in his estate including his inheritance is included to compile the surviving spouse's elective share.

49. Issue: Common law separate property

The correct answer is **D**. Absent fraud or undue influence, a property owner may leave all her property to whomever the property owner chooses, even over the objections of family members. This can be done by will A, or by a promise to will B (a contract to devise), or through a trust C.

50. Issue: Leasehold estate

The correct answer is **B**. Possession reverts back to the landlord. A, B, and C are transferred future interests.

51. Issue: Leasehold estate

The correct answer is **C**. Periodic tenancies are created when the landlord and tenant agree on a starting date for the leasehold to commence, but do not fix a termination date. They continue for successive time periods until one side gives notice. Because the rent is fixed at a monthly rate, it is a month-to-month tenancy. Had the rental been calculated on a yearly basis, a year-to-year tenancy would have been created. Had there been a specific termination date in the lease, the tenancy would have been a term of years A. If the lease could be terminated at the will of each party, it would have been a tenancy at will B or at sufferance D.

52. Issue: Periodic tenancy

The correct answer is **A**. Each party to the lease can terminate a periodic tenancy by giving notice, usually one time period in advance. Thus, in a month-to-month lease, either the landlord or the tenant can terminate by giving notice a month in advance, here on the fourth of each month. Automatic termination occurs only in a term of years at the end of the specified term B. Only tenancies at will or at sufferance can be terminated without notice C and D.

53. Issue: Death of tenant

The correct answer is **B**. A leasehold is a property right. At the tenant's death, the leasehold passes to the heirs or devisees of the tenant. Thus the son has inherited his father's tenancy, and may terminate it if he wishes in the same manner as could his father, as may the landlord. The death of the tenant does not terminate the lease A, nor does it constitute notice to terminate C.

54. Issue: Leasehold

The correct answer is **A**. Because both a starting and a termination date have been set a term of years has been created. That the stipulated term is less than a year does not matter. The lone issue is whether the lease specifies a fixed period. Periodic tenancies are created when the landlord and tenant agree on a starting date for the leasehold to commence, but do not fix a termination date C. They continue for successive periods until one side gives notice. Since the leasehold cannot be terminated at will, it is not a tenancy at will B or at sufferance D.

55. Issue: Term of years

The correct answer is **D**. Terms of years cannot be terminated prior to the expiration of the term (A through C). They expire at the termination date. Periodic tenancies allow termination with notice. At-will tenancies can be terminated at will.

56. Issue: Landlord's right to enter demised premises

The correct answer is **C**. By leasing the premises, the landlord has passed the right to possession to the tenant. His entry, without authorization in the lease or without the consent of the tenant, is a trespass, regardless of its minimal nature D. No rights to enter are "implied" (A and B). They must be express.

57. Issue: Leasehold

The correct answer is **B**. Because there is no fixed term or a period mentioned, and the lease provides the right to terminate at any time, a tenancy at will has been created.

58. Issue: Tenancy at will

The correct answer is **A**. Unlike other tenancies, the law regards the death of the tenant at will as a termination of the lease. Death ends the mutual volition that is required for a tenancy at will.

59. Issue: Implied promises in lease

The correct answer is **D**. Landlords promise that they have a right in the premises sufficient to create the leasehold estate (title) A and that they have not created a conflicting estate in another. They promise the right to possession B, and that they will not interfere with the tenant's interest (quiet enjoyment) C. Insurance is a matter for negotiation D.

60. Issue: Landlord delivering actual possession

The correct answer is **A**. The Uniform Residential Landlord and Tenant Act reverses the position in most American states that the landlord conveys only a right to possession rather than actual physical possession B. The issue is whether the landlord or the tenant should bear the expense of evicting a sitting tenant. At common law, most American jurisdictions did not place the burden on the landlord to make certain that a third party was not occupying the premises at the commencement of the lease. The exception was for short-term leases of furnished tenancies where immediate actual possession was implied D.

61. Issue: Lease purposes no longer attainable

The correct answer is **B**. If the purpose for which the tenant must use the premises as stated in the lease becomes no longer commercially viable, the tenant may be able to use the premises for other purposes under the contract law principle of commercial frustration. Only if the articulated purpose becomes illegal (like a brewery when Prohibition began) could the tenant argue impossibility A. Since the purpose is expressed in the lease, recourse to "implied warranties" is not likely. Here the premises are not "uninhabitable" D. The implied warranty of suitability is for non-residential (commercial) use, and generally relates to factors internal to the property, like faulty heating, cooling, etc. C.

62. Issue: Commercial frustration

The correct answer is **B**. To make a case for commercial frustration the tenant need not prove that the landlord acted in bad faith, that he knew that the limitation in the lease would render the premises unprofitable B. All the tenant need show is that it was not reasonably foreseeable at the time the lease was executed that use of the tenancy as an apartment would be unprofitable. The tenant need not demonstrate what the landlord knew A, C, or D.

63. Issue: Commercial frustration

The correct answer is **B**. The least costly means would be to reform the lease to allow the tenancy to be used as commercial property. The landlord continues to get the rent reserved. Of course, the tenant may get a windfall if commercial rents are higher than residential, which seems to be the case. Rescission is a possible remedy; this would allow the landlord to find another tenant, but if the residential use is not feasible, the landlord will probably only be able to get a commercial tenant A. The landlord would probably then get a windfall. The difference between the rent reserved and the fair market value of the premises as a residential apartment is probably the rent reserved if the residential purpose has been frustrated C. The difference between the rent reserved and the fair market value of the premises as a commercial building would give the tenant a windfall D.

64. Issue: Landlord's breach

The correct answer is **A**. The tenant might claim a constructive eviction, but she must move out. Whether she prevails is another matter. The tenant would argue that the landlord's failure to soundproof was a breach of the covenant of quiet enjoyment (or that the ad created an express warranty) that the landlord had an obligation to keep his tenants from disturbing each other. The noise level is probably not sufficient to render the premises uninhabitable B. Suitability is used in the commercial context D. The illegal lease remedy requires housing code violations that are probably not present here C.

65. Issue: Constructive eviction

The correct answer is **D**. For the tenant to prevail in a constructive eviction claim, the tenant must prove that the landlord had an obligation to act (here to quiet the neighbors), that the landlord breached that obligation, that the tenant made the landlord aware of the conditions (giving the landlord the opportunity to cure), and that the tenant moved out.

66. Issue: Constructive eviction

The correct answer is **D**. The actual loss suffered by the tenant is the benefit of the tenant's bargain: the difference between the rent of a similar apartment without the unruly neighbors over the term of the original lease with the landlord and the rent reserved. If the tenant rented at a favorable rate, or rents have increased, the tenant should be reimbursed for her increased costs. Relocation expenses are speculative and individual A; should the tenant stay at the Ritz while hunting for an alternative? Since the tenant does not have to pay the landlord the rent after the constructive eviction, the landlord should not pay the entire rental cost of the alternative accommodation B. The value of the premises to the tenant is likewise speculative C.

67. Issue: Implied warranty of habitability

The correct answer is **B**. Although the tenant might claim a constructive eviction, an actual eviction has not occurred; the landlord has not physically removed the tenant from the premises A. But room temperature at 90 degrees probably triggers an implied warranty of habitability claim. Suitability claims are used in the commercial context D. The illegal lease remedy requires housing code violations at the time the lease was executed: the air conditioner worked at that point C.

68. Issue: Implied warranty of habitability

The correct answer is **B**. It is only necessary for the tenant to prove that the defect is sufficiently serious to render the premises uninhabitable. The landlord need not have breached an express promise or obligation A; all residential leases imply habitability. The tenant need not quit the premises to bring an action C.

69. Issue: Implied warranty of habitability

The correct answer is **D**. Courts provide a variety of damages for breach of the implied warranty of habitability. The tenant could repair and deduct A. Or the tenant could claim that he should pay reduced rent, the fair rental value as is B; or have the rent reduced by the calculation of the difference between the rent reserved and the fair market value of the premises as habitable C. Relocation expenses are another matter D. They are too individualized and speculative.

70. Issue: Transfer

The correct answer is **C**. Because the transferee seems to be able to pay the rent, and engages in the same type of commercial enterprise as the current tenant, it seems as if the landlord is unreasonably refusing to consent. Even though the clause does not require the landlord's refusal to be reasonable, the law will imply it, and may not even permit the tenant to waive it.

71. Issue: Landlord's rights in sublease

The correct answer is **C**. The landlord can sue if he is in privity with the party in legal possession. If the landlord allows the tenant to assign, the landlord can sue both the tenant and the subtenant. The landlord is in privity of contract with the tenant, and privity of estate with the subtenant. But if there is a sublease, the landlord can only recover against the tenant A. There is neither privity of contract, nor privity of estate between the landlord and the subleasee. In neither case can the landlord raise the rent B and D absent the agreement of the tenant or the subtenant.

72. Issue: Landlord tort liability

The correct answer is **D**. At common law, landlord tort liability was limited to the three contexts enumerated in the question. Some courts have begun to extend landlord tort liability, but all jurisdictions recognize these three exceptions to the general rule.

73. Issue: Nuisance

The correct answer is **C**. English courts recognized it, but it never seems to have made the journey across the pond. All the others (A through C) did.

74. Issue: Nuisance

The correct answer is **C**. At common law, first in time gave first in right; response C would have been correct. However, under the Restatement, while first in time may be a factor that is considered, it is no longer dispositive. The Restatement defines a nuisance as an intentional B and unreasonable D invasion A by the actor of another party's interest in property.

75. Issue: Nuisance

The correct answer is **A**. B and C address whether there was an invasion. D is incorrect because though still a tort, the actor's conduct need not be considered wrongful for another property owner to prevail.

76. Issue: Nuisance

The correct answer is **D**. Because the factory likely provides many jobs and produces a product that is in demand, these factors probably outweigh the harm to a single householder C. However, the alternative Restatement test of unreasonable conduct is appropriate in this fact situation. Here the test is whether the actor can continue to operate the business and pay compensation to the householder. The factory would need to increase the price of bricks, and if it cannot do so it ought not to be a free rider, continuing operation while requiring Jones to suffer a loss of use value of her home. The noise and dust is just the non-trespassory invasion that the Restatement contemplates A. That the factory was first in time is of some relevance, but is not compelling B.

77. Issue: Nuisance

The correct answer is **B**. Many courts would award permanent damages in the amount of the decreased value of the homeowner's property. This is tantamount to a forced buy-out, and would allow the factory to continue to pollute, but since Jones would no longer own the house, it would not be a private nuisance to her. Awarding Jones an injunction would allow Jones to "hold up" the factory A. The owner would have to pay a premium in excess of Jones's actual lost value, because she could stop its entire operation. Whether she should get relocation expenses is debatable C, but in terms of efficiency it seems unnecessary; it's an added cost, and she moved to the nuisance.

78. Issue: Nuisance

The correct answer is **D**. Arguably the factory's good faith B and best efforts C are not an issue in nuisance law. A is totally irrelevant on its own. What matters is whether the noise is a sufficient non-trespassory invasion. That they cannot operate without creating noise may go to the issue of appropriate damages (permanent damages rather than injunction).

79. Issue: Servitudes

The correct answer is **B**. Both A and C are classic easements: interests in property held by a party that permits a party to do an affirmative act on another's property, an act which would otherwise constitute a trespass. In both cases, a vehicle owned by the holder can pass on the land of the land-holder. Answer D is an easement in gross; the personal right to enter onto the land of another to perform a particular act. At common law these were known as profits. Use restrictions are best classified as equitable servitudes, or if in writing and meeting particular requirements, real covenants B.

80. Issue: Easements by estoppel

The correct answer is **D**. When Smith authorized Jones to use his land for access, he created a license, authorization to use the property of another that is revocable at will by the licensor. But when Smith observed Jones making an investment in his land and in the improvement of the drive, the license became irrevocable: Smith was estopped from revoking. Easements by grant are created through the execution of a document A. Prescriptive easements are made by satisfying the requirements of adverse possession as modified to easements: open and notorious use, exclusive to others, continuous, and without the landholder's permission B. Easements by necessity C arise when land is divided into two or more parcels, not the case here.

81. Issue: Transferability of easements

The correct answer is **A**. When Smith sold the servient parcel (the land subject to the easement), the land still remained burdened if it was intended that the burden run with the land. Here, the type of easement suggests that the holder and the grantor would regard the interest as transferable: why else might Jones make the investment in improving the easement if it could be extinguished by sale C? While the benefit might run with Jones's parcel, and that is less clear from the facts, easements by estoppel are frequently considered personal to the original licensee, and endure only so long as is necessary to realize the cost of the investment made in reliance B.

82. Issue: Scope of easement

The correct answer is **A**. If the parties only contemplated individual use, then Smith might be able to enjoin guest use; but without explicit limitations, it is likely that occasional use by guests was in the contemplation of the parties. While previous unobstructed use by the guests might be evidence of the intent of the parties, it is not necessary to prove the contemplated use B. While easements may be personal and limited only to the individual to whom it was granted, courts would look to the circumstances; here there is no clear indication that it was so limited D.

83. Issue: Termination of servitudes

The correct answer is **A**. When Banks acquired Jones's parcel, he owned both the dominant and servient tenement. One cannot (and of course need not) have an easement in one's own land. Here, the holder of the servient interest also held the dominant interest. The easement was extinguished by merger. Even though Banks may have been using the drive, it was as a landowner of the drive, not as the holder of an easement. When he conveyed to Norris, he would have had to create the previous easement by granting it. This he did not do.

84. Issue: Overuse

The correct answer is **C**. Excessive use is use beyond the contemplated scope and can be enjoined. Here it is clear that the original license (which ripened into an easement) was for residential rather than commercial use. The easement should not be terminated unless of course the holder no longer contemplates residential use A and B. There has been no merger of the dominant and servient interests D.

85. Issue: Implied easements

The correct answer is **D**. Easements can be created by operation of law. When an owner of property subdivides her property in such a way as to render the conveyed parcel landlocked, the transferee has an easement by necessity. So unity of title, severance, and necessity are required A, B, and C. But there is no need to prove that the vendor used part of his land for the benefit of another (a quasi-easement), and that such use was apparent so that the owner of the servient tenement would be aware of the burden, a requirement for an easement by implication.

86. Issue: Negative easements/nuisance

The correct answer is **D**. This is the Restatement formulation of actionable nuisances. The shadowing is an "invasion." Modern nuisance law seems more appropriate than implying servitude law. Answers A and B are conceptualizations of servitudes that are not widely adopted in the United States. The spite fence analysis would prevail in traditional common law nuisance C.

87. Issue: Covenants

The correct answer is **A**. Here the promisee is suing the promisor. A simple contract action will do; no need to resort to covenants that run with the land. Where the promise is to be enforced against successors, then it must run. Use restrictions in transfers are best considered equitable servitudes or real covenants. Unless the grant expressly directs that the property return to the grantor B if the condition is broken or that the grantor may re-enter C, neither of which are specified in the restriction, there is no argument that he conveyed a defeasible fee. Though some courts refer to such limitations as negative easements, easements D are more usually affirmative interests to use the land of another.

88. Issue: Covenants

The correct answer is **D**. Again the parties to the dispute are the promisor and promisee, so no "property law" requirements are necessary.

89. Issue: Covenants that run with land/equitable servitudes

The correct answer is **A**. For Joe to sue Norris, Banks's promise must run with the land. Equitable servitudes were recognized by courts of equity in cases in which use restrictions could not be enforced at law against successors to the promisor's land. Since equity courts originally only allowed equitable remedies, the plaintiff could only ask for an injunction. Here Joe cannot sue Norris in contract since there was no privity of contract between them. Joe must prove intent that the promise runs with the land, and notice. Privity C and D is not necessary, though it may be used to prove notice. Mere intent to bind successors B is insufficient without notice of the promise to the successor of the promisor. Some courts, though not all, require that a promise touch and concern the land. Although the term is defined differently in different jurisdictions, the general rule is that the promise must provide some economic benefit to the land. Arguably it does because fewer bars may make bars more profitable, though one may also argue that the covenant makes the business more valuable, not the land per se.

90. Issue: Covenants that run with land/equitable servitudes

The correct answer is **C**. The elements of a real covenant are horizontal privity, vertical privity, and touch and concern. The restriction may meet the requirements of a real covenant. The promise was made to a seller from a buyer — it is in writing and in the deed. Banks came into ownership through a transfer from the promisor, so there is vertical privity. Some courts, though not all, still require that a promise touch and concern the land. Although the term is defined differently in different jurisdictions, the general rule is that the promise must provide some economic benefit to the land. Arguably it does because fewer bars may make bars more profitable, though one may also argue that the covenant makes the business more valuable, not the land per se. A is technically correct in some jurisdictions in which the remedies for equitable servitudes and real covenants are blended. D is incorrect because covenants not to compete can be enforced both at law for damages and in equity for an injunction. Privity is merely one of the requirements for a real covenant B.

91. Issue: Covenants that run with land/equitable servitudes

The correct answer is **A**. Most jurisdictions require that for a promise to bind the promisor's successors in an action for damages, the elements of a real covenant must be proved: the promise must be created by parties in horizontal privity (met here at least in some jurisdictions, since the promise was set out in a conveyance, though the early common law required mutual interests in land, and the stricter rule is not met here); the individual against whom the promise was to be enforced was in vertical privity with the promisor (met here because Norris bought from Banks); the promise touches and concerns the land (defined differently in different jurisdictions, but requiring some benefit — generally economic — to inure to the land, questionable here); and the parties intended the promise to run with the land (bind successors). Here there is no language in the covenant expressly binding future holders (and their heirs and assigns) A; it is possible that the court will find the covenant not to compete to benefit sufficiently Joe's land as opposed to his business C. Covenants are not always regarded as personal B, that is, enforceable only against the promisor. If the court did find intent that the covenant not to compete binds successors, and sufficient touch and concern, it would enforce the covenant against successors, not just against the promisor D, so long as Joe and Banks are in privity, and Banks and Norris are in privity. In this hypo, both the horizontal and vertical privity requirements are met.

92. Issue: Covenants that run with land/equitable servitudes

The correct answer is **B**. The successor in interest of the promisee can sue to enforce the promise as against successors of the promisor so long as it was intended that successors to the parcel benefited should also have the benefit of the promise. So if the requirements of an equitable servitude are met (probably), Moe can sue for an injunction. The real covenant is more doubtful because intent and touch and concern may be lacking. But if it were found Moe could also sue for damages.

93. Issue: Public use requirement

The correct answer is **D**. The Supreme Court of the United States (as opposed to some state supreme courts) defers to the legislative judgment as to the appropriate circumstances in which the takings power can be exercised under the "public use" requirement of the Fifth Amendment to the United States Constitution. So long as there is no bad faith in selecting the property to be taken, the legislature has wide latitude in determining what is a public use.

94. Issue: Rethinking the public use requirement

The correct answer is **A**. Justice O'Connor stressed that in defining a "public use" in circumstance in which the government did not occupy the land, the land acquired must be blighted, that is, it must contribute to the economic malaise that the urban renewal project sought to ameliorate. The circumstances listed in B through D were not present in *Kelo*.

95. Issue: Just compensation

The correct answer is **C**. Just compensation required by the Fifth Amendment is the fair market value (what a willing buyer would pay a willing seller) of the property and its fixtures. Since the government did not acquire the lost profits, or indeed profit from the move, it will not reimburse these costs. All of the other choices A, B, and D relate to the intrinsic value of the land.

96. Issue: Division of award for leased premises

The correct answer is **C**. The tenant's interest is property; so is the landlord's A and B. Under the "undivided fee rule," both interests are compensated. First the value of premises and fixtures is calculated. Then the value of the lease is calculated (difference between the fair rental value of the lease less the rent reserved for the term) and allocated to the tenant. The landlord receives the remaining value.

97. Issue: Takings by trespass

The correct answer is **C**. The Supreme Court (*Loretto v. Teleprompter*) has held that a permanent physical occupation of private land pursuant to government regulation triggers compensation even if the occupation is minimal. The degree of interference goes to the issue of the amount of compensation, not the need for it. Just compensation is not required where there is an average reciprocity of advantage A, because the landowner receives some tangible benefit for the loss occasioned by the regulation. In some situations, when the government exacts a concession there may be the need for compensation ("the unconstitutional condition"), but not where the ban on development would be justified B. Mere decrease in value is insufficient to always trigger compensation D.

98. Issue: Regulatory taking

The correct answer is **A**. It is not clear that one's primary expectations are necessarily fixed at the time of purchase. Smith has a plausible *Penn Central v. New York* argument that he planned to develop his lot, and that he has been deprived of the increased value of development. This is not a case for the application of *Lucas v. South Carolina Coastal Council*. In *Lucas*, the Supreme Court held that when a government regulation renders land valueless, not present here, the state's prohibition must be calculated to prevent a use that would have been a nuisance at common law B. If it did so act, it would not take away any development right, but merely preclude that which a landowner could not do, create a nuisance. But the Court in *Palazzolo v. Rhode Island* did not allow subdivision of property owned so as to create a part that is valueless. Thus the second lot cannot be regarded as valueless. There is no physical occupation D, nor has a short moratorium been considered a taking in *Tahoe-Sierra Preservation v. TRPA* C.

99. Issue: Regulatory taking

The correct answer is **A**. The government may only condition the granting of a permit upon some dedication of property if there is a close nexus between the loss to the public occasioned by the development and the dedication (*Nollan v. CCC*). Here the division permits a second house, and a second house does not have an appreciable effect on public access to the beach. If somehow it made access more difficult, the nexus would be satisfied. So the dedication required in the question might well be regarded as an unconstitutional condition. Because what has been required is the dedication of an easement and the easement is always there, there is a permanent cast to the exaction. But the public is not in permanent possession of his land C. His property is still valuable, and the use contemplated at purchase has not been forbidden B. The strip still has value D; he can use it.

100. Issue: Time, place, and manner restrictions

The correct answer is **A**. Even though the access right does make his land modestly less valuable D and the gate offers no average reciprocity of advantage because it does not benefit his land B, the fact that he can control access gives him the type of time, place, and manner controls that militate against finding the occupation a permanent one. He can regulate the use of the easement.

101. Issue: Takings jurisprudence

The correct answer is **B**. State law in these two cases prohibited the mining of coal so as to cause subsidence. *Loretto* and *Penn Central* are consistent, because in both the Court concedes that permanent physical trespasses are takings A. Likewise *Penn Coal v. Mahon* and *Penn Central* both use a "diminution in value" analysis to determine whether a regulation is a taking C. *Penn Central* and *Lucas* do diverge, but it is likely *Lucas* would have prevailed using the *Penn Central* analysis D.

102. Issue: *Euclid* rule

The correct answer is **B**. *Euclid v. Ambler Realty* did not consider whether as applied the zoning plan adopted by the Village was or was not a taking A and D. Nor did it expressly rule on whether the zoning board's plan may trigger compensation if it devalued land held by private owners C. It held only that a comprehensive zoning plan was a valid exercise or the police power, and therefore its use was not per se a taking.

103. Issue: Amortization of non-conforming uses

The correct answer is **D**. In fact, zoning boards are given wide latitude in allowing preexisting uses to continue as non-conforming uses after a change in zoning. The zoning board can make individualized decisions based on any of the factors so long as their judgments are reasonable and rational A, B, and C. But how far the store is to another store does not necessarily impact the zoned property and basing a denial on this factor may not be a rational judgment D.

104. Issue: Time, place, and manner restrictions

The correct answer is **D**. Although protected expression, the speaker and/or performer rights may be limited. Zoning regulations that limit venues where expression can be exercised are subject to intermediate scrutiny (*L.A. v. Alameda Books*). Instead of requiring the government to show that the regulation was the least restrictive means of limiting exercise (strict scrutiny) B or was predicated on a rational basis (that a reasonable legislature could find that the regulation is necessary to protect a public interest) C, the court requires some evidence that the regulation is targeted toward a particular permissible end, and is not gauged to impede expression because the content is objectionable.

105. Issue: Exclusionary zoning

The correct answer is **B**. The Supreme Court has allowed municipalities to determine what constitutes a family for the purposes of single family zoning ordinances (*Belle Terre v. Boraas*). The one exception is that multigenerational families must be considered as a single family. Answers A, C, and D pass the rational basis test.

106. Issue: Exclusionary zoning

The correct answer is **D**. The Supreme Court has not held such practices unconstitutional A. The Fair Housing Act does not address that issue either B. Led by the New Jersey Supreme Court in *Mount Laurel v. NAACP*, a few courts, but certainly not most C, have found the right to affordable housing protected by state constitutions.

107. Issue: Exclusionary zoning

The correct answer is **B**. The landowner must show that the granting of the ordinance would not thwart the comprehensive plan's aims A, and the welfare of the community will not be jeopardized. Both unique hardship B and unnecessary hardship D must be shown. But to show unique hardship the landowner need not show he is the only one adversely affected, just that the hardship is not generalized, that it does not affect most or all of the other properties in question.

108. Issue: Statute of Frauds

The correct answer is **A**. In order for an agreement for the sale of land to be enforced, the Statute of Frauds requires that it be in writing and signed by the party against whom it is to be enforced. Usually it is the sales contract that satisfies the statute, but a less formal instrument setting out the parties, the property, and the price satisfies the statute so long as it is signed B. A deposit is not a necessary requirement C. Smith has not satisfied the "part performance" exception D; he has not paid the price, entered, or improved the property.

109. Issue: Statute of Frauds

The correct answer is **C**. Had Jones cashed the check, the terms on the reverse substantially satisfy the parties, the property, and the price requirement of the statute; and had he cashed the check, assent to the terms might have been implied. The need for a signature would be waived. But he did not, so there is no acceptance of the terms (A and D). Receipt of the check B is not enough.

110. Issue: Statute of Frauds

The correct answer is **A**. Cashing the check might have been considered acceptance of Smith's offer. Likewise, had Smith entered the land without Jones's objection, there would have been sufficient part performance on his part to come within the exception of the statute. Neither full payment B nor the building contract C would be sufficient. However, had the builder entered with permission of vendor (and not without), there would have been acceptance D.

111. Issue: Statute of Frauds

The correct answer is **B**. Here there is an oral promise and reliance; equitable estoppel applies — the writing requirement is waived. Wholly gratuitous promises are not enforceable A; the price term, though not definite, is sufficiently ascertainable to be enforced C; and there seems to be a public policy interest rather than objection D to recognizing the contract.

112. Issue: Marketable title

The correct answer is **B**. Undisclosed restrictions on land render the title unmarketable. The single family dwelling restriction in the title, if undisclosed, renders the title unmarketable B. Although the agreement was to purchase residential land, "single family only" is a different restriction, and a narrower one. The existence of residential restrictions A is consistent with the contract; and zoning does not render the title unmarketable, because the buyer can enquire C. The title is still marketable even if the structures are not in conformity to law D. Marketability issues deal with land restrictions, not with fixtures. The buyer should have examined the building.

113. Issue: Marketable title

The correct answer is **A**. The misdescription in a title deed in the chain of title renders the title unmarketable. Each of the other choices does not render the title unmarketable. Only a guardian need execute the deed in the name of the minor titleholder B; so long as the will has been probated or an administration undertaken, an heir or legatee may transfer marketable title C; as may a corporate titleholder where the appropriate officer has executed the deed.

114. Issue: Risk of loss

The correct answer is **A**. Most jurisdictions recognize the doctrine of equitable conversion: the buyer (not the seller) D is deemed owner, and risk of loss passes to the buyer. The particularly dangerous nature of the property is not relevant B and C. If Smith had misrepresented, there might be some action for fraud, but it would not affect the outcome of action for specific performance.

115. Issue: Risk of loss

The correct answer is **A**. Equitable conversion will not be implemented if the parties agree to allocation of risk. Here they did. Whether there was insurance or not and which party held it should not be relevant. All that could be insured was the interest that the parties held in law. That Smith had it, B, doesn't change the doctrine's outcome; nor is Jones's belief about when she needed insurance coverage relevant C and D.